IMMORTALITY, RELIGION, *and* MORALS

BOOKS BY Ashley Montagu

Adolescent Sterility
The American Way of Life
The Anatomy of Swearing
Anthropology and Human Nature
The Biosocial Nature of Man
Coming into Being among the Australian Aborigines
The Cultured Man
Darwin, Competition, and Cooperation
The Direction of Human Development
Education and Human Relations
Edward Tyson, M.D., F.R.S. (1650–1708): And the Rise of Human and Comparative Anatomy in England
Handbook of Anthropometry
Human Heredity
The Human Revolution
The Humanization of Man
The Idea of Race
Immortality, Religion, and Morals
Introduction to Physical Anthropology
Life before Birth
Man: His First Two Million Years
Man in Process
Man Observed
Man's Most Dangerous Myth: The Fallacy of Race
The Natural Superiority of Women
On Being Human
On Being Intelligent
Prenatal Influences
Race, Science, and Humanity

The Reproductive Development of the Female
The Science of Man
Sex, Man, and Society
Statement on Race
Up the Ivy
Anatomy and Physiology (2 vols., with Edwin B. Steen)
The Dolphin in History (with John Lilly)
The Ignorance of Certainty (with Edward Darling)
Man's Evolution (with C. L. Brace)
The Prevalence of Nonsense (with Edward Darling)
Textbook of Human Genetics (with Max Levitan)

EDITOR

Atlas of Human Anatomy
The Concept of Race
The Concept of the Primitive
Culture and the Evolution of Man
Culture: Man's Adaptive Dimension
Genetic Mechanisms in Human Disease
International Pictorial Treasury of Knowledge
Man and Aggression
The Meaning of Love
Studies and Essays in the History of Science and Learning
Toynbee and History
The Human Dialogue (with Floyd W. Matson)

IMMORTALITY, RELIGION, and MORALS

by Ashley Montagu

HAWTHORN BOOKS, INC.
Publishers   New York

For Jennie and Van

Preface

THE FIRST three chapters of this book were delivered as lectures before the Ebenezer Butterick Foundation at the Brooklyn Institute of Arts and Sciences in New York on the evenings of the first, eighth, and fifteenth of March, 1951. The lectures were published under the title *Immortality* in 1955, and the little book has been out of print for several years. Since it appears to have met a real need, I have revised it quite extensively and have added five additional essays. Three of the latter deal with religion, one with morals and moralisms, and the final essay with the biosocial nature of man. The last essay, which was originally prepared for a UNESCO group, was included as an afterthought, with the intention of giving the reader an idea of the nature and problems of the creature who is so much concerned with being and existence.

The belief in immortality has for most people meant personal survival beyond death. In considering this belief, I have endeavored to show what functions it has served and to examine the motivations that have kept it alive. I have then gone on to consider the kind of immortality in which a modern man can believe.

In the remaining essays religion, morals, and moralisms are discussed from an anthropological point of view, with the object of assisting the interested reader toward a clearer understanding of those various devices by which men have attempted to meet their most important problems.

A. M.

Princeton, New Jersey

Acknowledgments

The author gratefully thanks the following publishers for permission to quote from the works published by them:

Chatto & Windus, London, Gordon Bottomley and Denys Harding (editors), *The Collected Poems of Isaac Rosenberg*

Harcourt, Brace & World, Sylvia Anthony, *The Child's Discovery of Death*

The Hogarth Press, Sigmund Freud, *The Future of an Illusion*

The Macmillan Company, Donald Attwater (editor), *A Catholic Dictionary*

The Macmillan Company, Herbert Dingle, *Science and Human Experience*

The Macmillan Company, James G. Frazer, *The Belief in Immortality*

The Macmillan Company, F. C. S. Northrop, *The Meeting of East and West*

University of North Carolina Press, Bronislaw Malinowski, *A Scientific Theory of Culture*

University of Toronto Press, Edmund Carpenter, *Explorations*

Yale University Press, Ernst Cassirer, *An Essay on Man*

Contents

Happy are they which live
not in that disadvantage of time,
when men could say little for
futurity, but from reason.

—Sir Thomas Browne,
Hydriotaphia, 1658

From too much love of living,
  From hope and fear set free,
We thank with brief thanksgiving
  Whatever gods may be
That no life lives for ever;
  That dead men rise up never;
That even the weariest river
  Winds somewhere safe to sea.

—A. C. Swinburne,
The Garden of Proserpine

Who comes?
Is it the hound of dawn approaching?
Away,
Or I will harness you to my team.

—Aivilik Eskimo song

IMMORTALITY, RELIGION, *and* MORALS

Biology and Immortality

The blazing evidence of immortality is our dissatisfaction
with any other solution.
— Ralph Waldo Emerson, *Journal*, July, 1855

MAN, WE may reasonably assume, is the only living creature
who entertains the idea of immortality. In any event, even
though we have no idea what other animals may think upon
the matter, we shall here perforce be concerned with man's
conception of immortality and its significance for living
human beings. Furthermore, our discussion will be restricted
to discussing those aspects of the subject about which we
have knowledge, remembering the words of Sir James Frazer,
that "Of all the many forms which natural religion has assumed none probably has exerted so deep and far-reaching an
influence on human life as the belief in immortality and the
worship of the dead"; hence, a discussion

of this momentous creed and of the practical consequences
which have been deduced from it can hardly fail to be at
once instructive and impressive, whether we regard the
record with complacency as a noble testimony to the aspiring

genius of man, who claims to outlive the sun and the stars, or whether we view it with pity as a melancholy monument of fruitless labour and barren ingenuity expended in prying into that great mystery of which fools profess their knowledge and wise men confess their ignorance.[1]

It is a good thing, every so often, to define for ourselves as clearly as we are able what we think we understand by certain of our ideas or beliefs. Perhaps it would be appropriate at this point to define for ourselves what we understand by the idea or belief in immortality. It is precisely at this juncture that the true philosopher would look forward to a regular field day, for the idea of immortality has meant many different things to many people, so that the mere recital of the variety of forms the idea has assumed would fill volumes. We shall forgo that exercise here. It is the theme with which we are concerned, not the variations.

The belief in immortality is most generally expressed in the idea that when the life of a human being comes to an end on this earth, it is for him as a person continued in another world or worlds or in this world in some other form. The first version of the belief is the belief in immortality pure and simple, and the second version of the belief is the belief in reincarnation.

The numerous forms the belief in immortality has taken, particularly among nonliterate peoples, is a subject that has been treated by several scholars, but most notably by Sir James Frazer in his Gifford lectures (1911–12), *The Belief in Immortality*. All who are interested in the anthropology of the subject may most profitably be referred to Frazer's magisterial study. Here we may most usefully accept the simplest and shortest definition of immortality as the belief in life after death. But here, once more, we find ourselves pulled up short, for this definition assumes that we know what both life and death are, and as Confucius (551–478 B.C.) pointed out, if we do not understand the one how can we understand the other? "Where I am, death is not," said Epicurus. "When death is, I am not." Therefore we can never have anything to do with death.

Let us define life as the state of an organism in which it is capable of performing its functions. And let us define death as the state of termination of the organism's capacity to perform its functions.

And what are the *functions* of life from the standpoint of the biologist? Those functions are: (1) the ability to respond to stimuli (*irritability*), (2) the ability to move (*motility*), (3) the ability to regulate itself (*homeostasis*), and (4) the ability to reproduce (*multiplication*). As we shall see in the development of our theme, the criteria of this biological development of life are intimately bound up with the conception of immortality that will be developed in these pages; for in what follows we shall be concerned with immortality *and* life, with immortality as a function of human beings in search of a harmonic, gratifying way of life.

In short, in these pages I shall endeavor to develop a social biologist's view of the meaning and the function of the idea of immortality for living human beings. Let us begin with a consideration of the biological facts.

THE BIOLOGICAL FACTS

All living things come into being from other living things. This is a statement of a basic biological phenomenon. At the same time it is a statement of the fact of immortality. Most human beings who have believed in immortality have been quite unaware of this fundamental fact and have supported and embroidered their beliefs entirely and altogether apart from such *conscious knowledge*. I would here underscore the words "conscious knowledge," for there exists suggestive evidence that indicates the possible existence in every human being of an unconscious awareness of this biological fact. Goethe, for example, seems to have felt this. He said in conversation with Chancellor von Müller:

> It would be thoroughly impossible for a thinking being to think of a cessation of thought and life. Everyone carries the proof of immortality within himself, and quite involuntarily. But just as soon as a man tries to step outside of himself and become objective, just as soon as a man wants to prove or wants to understand personal survival dogmatically, and in a narrow way make that inner perception clear to himself, then he loses himself in contradictions.

We may begin our discussion with the single-celled or unicellular organism. At a certain stage in its growth the unicellular organism undergoes certain changes that may be measured at its membranous surface—such as a change in surface tension, a change that expresses something of the degree of pressure within the cell. At such a time the organism tends to reduplicate itself, that is, to reproduce. The net effect of this activity is that its own tension is reduced and another organism like itself comes into being. Were we to leave the description of the complex and significant events that occur during the process of reproduction at so crass a level, we should altogether miss the tremendous significance of probably the most important series of events that occur in the life of every organism, from the single-celled to the multicellular consisting, like the human organism, of trillions of cells. Let us recall once more that every form of life comes into being from some other life, that all cells originate from other cells, *omnis cellula e cellula.*

Whatever the mode of reproduction, whether it be asexual or sexual, by budding or fission, the same basic pattern is maintained throughout the living kingdom. The parental cell or cells contribute materials to the cell, which they in their turn had derived from their genitor or genitors. It was August Weismann (1834–1914), the great German biologist, who first spoke of "the continuity of the germ plasm," and it was he who spoke of "the immortality of unicellular beings and of the reproductive cells of multicellular organisms."[2] Weismann pointed out that the immortality of unicellular organisms and of germ cells is not absolute, but potential. Such organisms, Weismann made clear, can, and the majority of cases do, die, but a part of each lives on. Weismann asked the rhetorical question, "But is it one and the same substance that continues to live? Does not life, here and everywhere else, depend on assimilation, that is, on a constant change of material? What then is immortal?" And Weismann answered:

Apparently not a substance at all, but a certain form of motion. The protoplasm of unicellular beings possesses such an arrangement in its chemical and molecular structure, that the cycle of material which makes up life is ever repeating itself, and can always begin afresh so long as the external conditions remain favourable. In this respect it may be compared to the circulation of water on the earth. Water evaporates, is condensed into cloud, falls to the earth as rain, only once more to evaporate, and thus the cycle repeats itself. And just as there exists no inherent cause in the physical and chemical nature of water, which interrupts this circulation, so in the physical nature of the protoplasm of unicellular beings there is nothing which puts an end to the cycle of existence—that is fission, growth by assimilation, and then fission again.[3]

What Weismann means by "a certain form of motion" we would today, more than seventy years later, call the energy relations of the atoms constituting the chromosomal and extrachromosomal particles that set the limits to the kind of organism that will develop. Within the limits thus set an enormous amount of variability is possible, a variability rendered possible as a result of the chromosomal and extrachromosomal mechanism, which is set in motion during cell reproduction and the transmission of the chromosomes and other parts of the germ cells to the newly forming organism. The body or somatic cells ultimately die, but the germ cells function to create other organisms, transmitting to them a system of molecular structures or energy relations or chemical packages, which are characterized by the power to repeat the process in an endless cycle and by means of the sexual process with a tremendous range of variability.

Writing in 1890, Weismann remarked:

> We have hitherto been without a scientific conception of immortality: we must understand by this term—not life without beginning or end—but life which, when is has once originated, continues without limit, accompanied or unaccompanied by modification (viz. specific changes in unicellular organisms, or in the germ-plasm of multicellular forms). This immortality is a movement of organic material, which always recurs in a cycle, and is associated with no force that tends to arrest its progress, just as the motion of planets is associated with nothing that tends to arrest their movement, although it had a beginning and must at some future time, by the operation of external causes, come to an end.[4]

Astronomers and geologists tell us that the end will not be for a very long time to come,[5] and physicists assure us that when it comes it will be a transformation of energy from one complex series of forms to another. The world will suffer a change, ceasing to exist in its present form, and will be transmuted into some other organization of atoms.

The law of conservation of energy, which states that energy is neither created nor destroyed in any of its transformations, and the fact of the continuity of the germ plasm constitute a scientific basis for the belief in both the indestructibility of energy or matter and the imperishability of life—in other words, the basis for our belief in the immortality of different levels of integration of energy relations. As Longfellow says:

> Nothing that is shall perish utterly,
> But perish only to revive again.
> In other forms...

The idea of the ultimate, complete annihilation of this world is something that most human beings have found both inconceivable and intolerable.[6] But if the authorities are to be believed, this will ultimately be the case, and the idea of immortality constitutes a rod upon which to lean in the belief that whatever may happen to the world, one's self, one's soul, will remain indestructible. The position was well expressed by Darwin. He wrote:

> With respect to immortality, nothing shows me [so clearly] how strong and almost instinctive a belief it is, as the consideration of the view now held by most physicists, namely, that the sun with all the planets will in time grow too cold for life,[7] unless indeed some great body dashes into the sun, and thus gives it fresh life. Believing as I do that man in the distant future will be a far more perfect creature than he now is, it is an intolerable thought that he and all other sentient beings

are doomed to complete annihilation after such long-continued slow progress. To those who fully admit the immortality of the human soul, the destruction of our world will not appear so dreadful.[8]

We see, then, as Weismann was the first to point out, that though the individual and his particular body cells may "perish utterly" his germ cells will, in reproduction, maintain the continuity of life, imperishably, immortally. And so, the immortality of life. But this is to demonstrate the immortality of the germ plasm, "the physical basis of life," as Thomas Henry Huxley called it. What of those further related facts that from the biological standpoint may throw some additional light for us on the basic nature of the belief in immortality? What of that possibly unconscious biological basis for the belief in immortality to which I have previously alluded?

Let us return to the consideration of the single cell, whether it be of a unicellular or of a multicellular organism. As a result of metabolic changes during the growth of the cell at a certain stage of its development, the cell reduplicates itself, reproduces itself. What occurs during the process of reproduction is most important. At the inception of cell division the protoplasm of the cell begins to flow into the adjacent field, and invaginations appear at opposite poles of the cell membrane. The chromosomes split longitudinally into a set of exact replicas of themselves, as does every part of the nucleus in which they are contained, as well as the extranuclear materials. During this period there is an appreciable interval of time during which the cell that is coming into being is dependent upon the maternal cell for its continuing functions, and both are in an interdependent relationship to each other, so that whatever happens to the one affects the other. The two organisms were originally one, and the one gradually produces another. During the process of reproduction the parental cell and the offspring cell are enclosed within a single membrane. The one continues the life of the other, and the other is a continuation of the life of the genitor.

Now, what I am suggesting here is that it is this process of reproduction, this process of interdependency and dependency, that is associated with a certain patterning of the organic molecules involved, which have something of the character of memory. The organism, it is suggested, remembers its original state of dependency upon and interdependency with another organism. Nothing in the nature of a determinate, conscious act of memory is suggested, but rather that inherent in the process of reproduction there is a certain patterning and arrangement of molecules, which are maintained in a balanced relationship between the two organisms, which inevitably becomes a part of the filial organism and constitutes for it a mnemic or memory system of the early events as an inseparable part of the tissues of the organism. Today we know that memory is a capacity of all living tissues. But it must be repeated: I am not suggesting that living tissues consciously remember in any way resembling the sense of cerebral memory, but rather in the sense worked out by Professor Richard Semon in his book *The Mneme*[9]—in other words, through those enduring, primarily latent modifications produced in living cells by stimuli. Such modifications were called, by Semon, *engrams*. The effect that remains in the stimulated *cell* after the excitement produced by the stimulus has ceased is the engram, and the capacity for such aftereffects that living cells possess is called *mneme*. In this mnemic sense the organism unconsciously remembers its original state of dependency and interdependency and is forever seeking the proximity of other organisms in order to obtain the satisfactions to be derived from association. For association confers survival benefits upon those engaged in it, and benefits of a more immediate nature accrue to the participants.[10] I am here suggesting that it is this predilection for that association that is inherited from the manner of our own origin in association with our maternal genitors that constitutes the unconscious biologically derived basis of our desire for continued association with our fellow human beings, and even much loved domestic animals, after our capacities for association have come to an end upon this earth.

The death of those we love is experienced as both unpardonable and unacceptable. This side of despair there rises up in the breast the hope, the expectation, that somewhere, sometime, we shall be reunited. Such a state of mind may not constitute the origin of the belief in immortality, but clearly that state of mind powerfully contributes to the hold of that belief upon mankind.

Life is too short, and death is the one reality in which men cannot believe, even though they know that all men must die, that all are under sentence of death. Hence, the engagement and vanquishing of death by religion. "O death, where is thy sting? O grave, where is thy victory?" It was beautifully put in a World War I song, sung by the British soldiers on the Western front to an old Salvation Army tune:

The bells of hell go ting-a-ling-a-ling for you and not for me.
For me the angels sing-a-ling-a-ling, They've got the goods for me.
O death where is thy sting-a-ling-a-ling? O grave thy victory?
The bells of hell go ting-a-ling-a-ling, for you and not for me.

I have already quoted Goethe, and most men have felt similarly. An outstanding and representative statement of the power of the belief in immortality was made by no less a person than Frederick Barnard (1809–89), distinguished scientist and educator and from 1864 to 1889 president of Columbia University (Columbia College, as it then was). In 1873 Barnard declared that if spontaneous generation, organic evolution, and the correlation of mental and physical forces were true, then the existence of God and the immortality of the soul were impossible. To him this was an irreconcilable and unendurable situation, and therefore to preserve his dream of heaven he renounced his intellectual integrity, stating his position in words that surely describe the stand so many other men have taken:

> Much as I love truth in the abstract I love my sense of immortality still more; and if the final outcome of all the boasted discoveries of modern science is to disclose to men that they are more evanescent than the shadow of the swallow's wing upon the lake . . . if this, after all, is the best that science can give one, give me then, I pray, no more science. I will live on in my simple ignorance, as my father did before me; and when I shall at length be sent to my final repose, let me . . . lie down to pleasant, even though they may be deceitful, dreams.

Apparently President Barnard thought those dreams anything but deceitful. The strength of belief or certitude is no proof of certainty, and it is rather simple-minded to suggest that because men have felt certain about life after death there must be such a thing. It may, however, be reasonably suggested that there are some facts that lend themselves to the interpretation I am trying to give them, namely, that there is a biological basis for the will to believe in immortality in the pleasure derived from the society of one's fellows, which pleasure in turn is derived from the original social situation in the reproductive process and in the desire to continue that social situation indefinitely.

In spite of the scorn a critic of naturalism[11] has poured upon Malinowski's statement that "survival after death is probably one of the earliest mystical hypotheses, related perhaps to some deep biological cravings of the organism,"[12] it will be perceived that I could not be more in agreement than I am with Malinowski's statement. And yet, our critic, Professor Eliseo Vivas, tells us that he does not believe "that we could find a reputable psychologist who would take seriously such biological cravings." I should not like to think that Professor Vivas really means this, for there are many reputable psychologists who take such cravings seriously, among them Erich Fromm, Abraham Maslow, and Gardner Murphy. Nothing human should be alien to the student of man, and every thinker worth his salt should view knowledge in the Whiteheadian sense, as exploration.

Having now, like a good philosopher, added yet another theory in exploration and in explanation of man's will to believe in immortality, but this time from the uncustomary viewpoint of a social biologist, let us proceed from the continuing standpoint of the social biologist to a discussion of the body-mind problem insofar as it relates to our discussion of immortality.

THE BODY-MIND PROBLEM

Let it at once be said that the body-mind problem is a spurious problem, even more so than the heredity-environment problem. The body-mind dichotomy we owe principally to Plato and its naturalization by the early Church Fathers in the Western world. A human being is an organism, that is to say, an organization of physicochemical structures organized to function integratively in a variety of adaptive ways. An organism is an acting system, that is to say, a behaving system. Any act of an organism is behavior, and behavior is a synonym for mind. What the organism does is mind. But an organism, a living organism, is *doing*, therefore an organism is mind. To speak of body and mind as if they were separate and separable things is to introduce separation where separation does not exist and where it is impossible to produce such a separation. Mind is an abstraction from behavior. There is no such thing as body and mind, there is only a living organism, and what is called "mind" is but an aspect of its functioning. Similarly, the separation between "structure" and "function" is quite arbitrary. Structure and function are wholly interdependent processes, the organism forming itself structurally by function and functioning through its form.[13] As Dr. L. Monné has pointed out, "structure and function of protoplasm are intimately correlated with each other. Any function is accompanied by regular changes of the structure of protoplasm on the microscopical, submicroscopical and stereoscopical levels."[14] To quote a distinguished biological authority, Professor Edmund W. Sinnott: "In any living system one cannot separate the processes of growth which lead to the development of the body from those by which the life of the body is maintained."[15] From the philosophical standpoint Professor Gilbert Ryle has recently thoroughly dissected and anatomized the body-mind fallacy. The interested student may be referred to his admirable book.[16] The consensus of modern scientific opinion may be summed up in the words of the eminent neuroanatomist, Professor Gerhardt von Bonin, to wit, that "the mind does not go 'more ghostly than a ghost' but rather goes as do the neurons of the brain,"[17] and that with William James, Russell, and Carnap, all that can be called mind constitutes a pattern of relations.

Recent researches in neurophysiology support to the hilt Professor Roy W. Sellars' remark that mind as well as body are ultimately one and have but secondary endurance and will perish. But when Professor Sellars remarks that "it is upon this rock that all theories of immortality break to pieces,"[18] we may perhaps question the universal "all." I can see nothing upon which the theory of the immortality of life, which is exemplified by the fact of the continuity of the germ plasm, can break to pieces. Undoubtedly Professor Sellars had in mind theories relating to the immortality of the personal soul as a separable entity from the body. Here, I cannot but be in full agreement with Professor Sellars. If, with C. A. Strong, we identify the "soul" with the self,[19] there remains an important sense in which the soul may be said, at least in part, to survive the death of the body. The soul as an enduring entity in itself ceases to be at death, but its effects may endure eternally as a consequence of the behavior of the person—for the soul, the self, is the functioning organization of all that a person is—and all a person is, the self, he has largely acquired from other selves. Failure to incorporate what he has learned from other selves into his own organism would result in an individual without a self, without a soul.[20]

C. A. Strong says that "What really is lodged in the body is the nervous system, which in its intrinsic nature is the soul; the soul, or nervous system, and the rest of the body are the real duality."[21]

But in point of fact there is no duality here. The duality arises only when one fails to understand that the whole body is nothing but a nervous system. The whole organism is a nervous system, and in C. A. Strong's terms, therefore, the whole body in its intrinsic nature is the soul—but in our terms only when that body has been organized in the energy field of human social relations. A nervous system that is part or potential of a member of the species *Homo sapiens* does not become human unless it is organized in a human manner in a human environment. Nervous processes constitute the human soul. The nervous system interacts with the world of experience, and so does the self. Between the self and the nervous process, C. A. Strong says, there is no interaction, but only a strict parallelism, because the nervous process is a perceptual rendering of the self. Again, this dualism seems quite unnecessary to me, and one may perceive that it is because philosophers have fragmented themselves into different sense organs that they are constrained to think in this atomistic, nonunitary manner. Psychophysical parallelism is the old body-mind dichotomy in very thin disguise. The nervous process *is* the behavior—and not merely its parallel accompaniment. Whether perceived as physiological or psychological, the nervous process remains the same.

Unless this world and our experience in it be but a dream[22]—which may be doubted—and we are destined to wake up in some other world of reality, I cannot but see that the notion of a physical soul surviving after death is forever shattered. For if body and soul are one, then death of the body means death of the soul. We can be reasonably certain that if there are any other habitable worlds human souls do not journey to them.

Do men, then, at death vanish into husks and the formless ruin of oblivion? Physically, yes. Culturally, no. We know that what men have done during their lives, the good *and* the evil, lives after them, to influence other human beings in consonance with the power of their ideas and their deeds.[23]

NOTES

[1] Sir James G. Frazer, *The Belief in Immortality*, Vol. 1 (London: Macmillan, 1913), pp. vii–viii.

[2] August Weismann, *Essays upon Heredity*, Vol. 2 (Oxford: Clarendon Press, 1892), p. 74.

[3] *Ibid.*, p. 75.

[4] *Ibid.*, p. 79.

[5] The latest estimate is 10,000,000,000 years. See Fred Hoyle, *The Nature of the Universe* (New York: Harper and Row, 1951), p. 131. Calculating at the rate of thirty years for a human generation, it may easily be determined that man has another three and a half billion generations—approximately—before the surface of the earth becomes too hot to support life. By that time, however, man may have devised a means of safely removing himself to another galaxy.

[6] That is, in the pre–atom bomb world. In the world of the hydrogen and cobalt bombs human beings no longer find the idea of complete annihilation of this world either inconceivable or intolerable. Most persons have adopted an attitude of resignation to the inevitable—whatever it may prove to be. Such apathy is more dangerous than any atom bomb.

[7] Contemporary astrophysical opinion holds that instead of growing cooler the earth will ultimately grow too hot for life to be able to continue. See Hoyle, *op. cit.*

[8] *The Life and Letters of Charles Darwin*, ed. by Francis Darwin and A. C. Seward, Vol. 1 (London: John Murray, 1888), p. 312.

[9] Richard Semon, *The Mneme* (New York: Macmillan, 1921).

[10] C. Warder Allee, *Cooperation Among Animals* (New York: Schuman, 1951).

[11] Eliseo Vivas, *The Moral Life and the Ethical Life* (Chicago: University of Chicago Press, 1950), p. 195.

[12] Bronislaw Malinowski, *A Scientific Theory of Culture* (Chapel Hill: University of North Carolina Press, 1944), p. 174.

[13] See G. L. Freeman, *Physiological Psychology* (New York: Van Nostrand, 1948).

[14] L. Monné, "Structure and Function of Neurones in Relation to Mental Activity," *Biological Reviews*, Vol. 24 (1949), pp. 297–315.

[15] E. W. Sinnott, *Cell and Psyche* (Chapel Hill: University of North Carolina Press, 1950), p. 60.

[16] Gilbert Ryle, *The Concept of Mind* (New York: Barnes and Noble, 1949). See also Peter Laslett (ed.), *The Physical Basis of Mind* (New York: Macmillan, 1950).

[17] Gerhardt von Bonin, *Essay on the Cerebral Cortex* (Springfield, Ill.: Charles C. Thomas, 1950), p. x.

[18] Roy Wood Sellars, *The Philosophy of Physical Realism* (New York: Macmillan, 1932), p. 304.

[19] C. A. Strong, "The Soul and Its Bodily Presentment," in *Essays on the Natural Origin of the Mind* (London: Macmillan, 1930), p. 160.

[20] For an admirable discussion of the self from an anthropological point of view see A. I. Hallowell, "The Self and Its Behavioral Environment," *Explorations*, Vol. 2 (University of Toronto, 1954), pp. 106–65.

[21] *Ibid.*, p. 186.

[22] F. C. S. Schiller, "Plato's Phaedo and the Ancient Hope of Immortality," in *Our Human Truths* (New York: Columbia University Press, 1939), pp. 153–54.

[23] Again an artificial dissociation, for ideas are deeds; ideas are acts of the organism, behavior.

CHAPTER 2

The Belief in Immortality

Can death be sleep, when life is but a dream
And scenes of bliss pass as a phantom by?
The transient pleasures as a vision seem,
And yet we think the greatest pain's to die.
—John Keats, *On Death*

IN THE preceding pages the belief in immortality from the standpoint of a social biologist has been considered and it is suggested that from such a viewpoint there is some reason to believe that there is possibly a biological basis for the belief in the drive to form and maintain associations with one's fellows. It was not intended to suggest that this was the only ground for the belief.

Why do men believe in immortality? It is with the answer to this question that we shall be concerned in this chapter.

WHY DO MEN BELIEVE IN IMMORTALITY?

The belief in immortality is probably as old as man, and man is several million years old. For prehistoric man, probably everything about him was alive, and death constituted but a translation from one form of being to another. The first evidence we have of religious beliefs in man are derived from the burial customs of Neanderthal man. Neanderthal man flourished during the third interglacial period, which commenced about 150,000 years ago, and also during the fourth glacial period, which came to an end about 25,000 years ago. The Neanderthal men buried their dead, usually within the cave that had, presumably, been their home during life. To this day there are some peoples who bury the corpse within the house or domain; burial in the home grounds or chapel attached to or within the house has persisted to the present. Shall we be far wrong in assuming the motive for this practice to be the desire to retain the mortal remains of the loved one as closely as possible and that this was the motive of Neanderthal man as well as of many other men down to the present day? Perhaps not the only motive, but possibly one among several.

It may be thought by some that there is one obvious reason why burial would suggest itself as the best way of dealing with a corpse, namely, the putrefaction that sets in shortly after death. The fact is, however, that the communities of Stone Age man were very small, and leaving a corpse out in the open would have been by far the most comfortable and easiest way of disposing of it. Indeed, there are many peoples who at the present day ceremonially dispose of their dead by simple exposure in the open, by tree burial as among the Australian aborigines, and on the open ground as in Yucatan.[1]

Miss Effie Bendann, who has made a study of death customs and burial rites, has shown that the importance attached to disposal of the dead is universal. The principle is invariably the same—the dead would "walk" unless the body were disposed of with the appropriate ceremony. The natural tendency, so it is believed, for those who have died is to find their way back to the places that have been their haunts during life. The earliest recorded statement of this belief is to be found in the Babylonian *Epic of Gilgamesh*, the first great work of its kind in the poetry of the human race of which we have any record. This poem was written some 4000 years ago. In the relevant passage, depicting the lot of those whose spirit remains at rest because they have received appropriate burial, reference is made to the awful fate of those who are denied fitting burial:

> But he whose corpse remains in the field
> As you and I have seen,
> His spirit has no rest on the earth,
> The one whose spirit is not cared for by anyone,
> As you and I have seen,
> He is consumed by gnawing hunger, by a longing for food
> That is left on the street he is obliged to eat.[2]

If Neanderthal men buried their dead for a similar reason, then it would be clear that they believed in the persistence of the soul after death, that they believed in immortality. By inference we know this to be almost certainly true of the men of Aurignacian times, who lived between 20,000 and 15,000 years ago. These people ceremonially interred their dead, furnishing them with implements and food with which to assist them to make the journey to the other world, and in many cases they placed red ochre within the grave, presumably as a symbol of the life-giving properties of blood.

   Almost certainly the belief in immortality is of considerable antiquity. What is it that in most, if not in all, human communities causes men to develop and cling to the belief in perpetual life in a hereafter? Let us give ear to the words of that wise man, Sir Thomas Browne, writing in the middle of the seventeenth century. He says in his exquisite *Hydriota-phia or Urne-Buriall,*

> It is the heaviest stone that melancholy can throw at a man, to tell him he is at the end of his nature; or that there is no further state to come, unto which this seemes progressional, and otherwise made in vain; Without this accomplishment the natural expectation and desire of such a state, were but a fallacy in nature. Unsatisfied Considerators would quarrel the justice of their constitutions, and rest content that Adam had fallen lower, whereby knowing no other Original, and deeper ignorance of themselves, they might have enjoyed the happiness of inferior Creatures who in tranquility possess their constitutions, as having not the apprehension to deplore their own natures. And being framed below the circumference of these hopes, or cognition of better being, the wisdom of God hath necessitated their contentment, will be able at last to tell us we are more than our present selves; and evacuate such hopes in the fruition of their own accomplishments.[3]

Yes, "we are more than our present selves," and that there is "a further state to come," that we are not "such stuff/As dreams are made on, and our little life/. . . [but] rounded with a sleep." I think it may be granted that Sir Thomas Browne has named two of the principal ideas that supply some at least of the motivation for the belief in immortality.

It is difficult for men to conceive the possibility of ceasing to be, since the past is but a symbol and the future a reality compounded of the present: "This life cannot be all they swear/For how unpleasant if it were." How can one believe that death is "Only the sleep eternal/In an eternal night"? Indeed, to most men who have lived, it is a safe guess that the possibility has never occurred. It would seem to be a possibility that rarely occurred to men up to the very recent period. As Sir James Frazer has pointed out, among nonliterate peoples—the so-called primitive peoples of the earth—the belief in immortality is not a speculation or conjecture of hope or fear; it is a practical certainty "which the individual as little dreams of doubting as he doubts the reality of his conscious existence."[4] In a passage, part of which I have already quoted, Malinowski wrote:

> Survival after death is probably one of the earliest of mythical hypotheses, related perhaps to some deep biological cravings of the organism, but certainly contributing to the stability of social groups and towards the sense that human endeavors are not as limited as purely rational experience shows. Ideas which, on the one hand, assert that man can control some elements of chance, and on the other hand, imply that in nature itself, there is a benevolent or vindictive response to human activities, contain the germs of more highly developed concepts, such as Providence, a moral sense in creation, and the goal of human existence.[5]

"Life," as Sir Thomas Browne says, "is a pure flame, and we live by an invisible Sun within us." But Sir Thomas Browne was convinced that that flame is extinguished forever with death. Man has been likened to a lighted candle, which stands erect throwing light all about it, at the cost of its own consumption. Man's burning substance is consumed, the light flickers and goes out, and there is no more light, only eternal darkness. But this truth, if it be a truth, men cannot accept. And if reason is against a man, man will be against reason. "Ready," as Browne says, "to be anything, in the extasie of being ever." "Purely rational experience" is of no great moment here, for the desire for immortality in men has in the past been so strong that they have accepted it without either depending upon or requiring the demonstrations of rational experience. Even Plato is so anxious to believe in immortality that in several of his works, but most notably in *The Phaedo*, he attempts to use every possible argument to demonstrate the truth of immortality to himself. If we are to judge of his success by the quality of his arguments, we must conclude that he failed to convince both himself and his readers. And that is the point: The belief in immortality is ultimately an act of faith, whatever its origins and whatever its end, and faith is untouchable. It cannot be demonstrated as a fact. Faith is the belief in the substance of things to come. But as Professor Abraham Edel has remarked,

> questions about immortality are not well answered merely by showing that all perceptible consequences that could be deduced from the hypothesis that Mr. A. now is a disembodied spirit are not verified or are unverifiable. They are better answered by examining the content of the idea until it appears as the demand for a richer quality of life in the context of collective insecurity engendered by lack of control over nature and the conflicts of man against man.[6]

This, as Professor Edel says, is the way it looks to a philosophical materialist, and among some men living in the communities of the Western world, I should think that personal rather than collective insecurity, from whatsoever causes arising, would make fertile soil in which the firm plant of immortality could grow. The psychoanalysts are on firm ground when they point out that the pleasure-seeking id[7] is concentrated on living, *not* dying (in spite of Freud's purely mythical "death instinct"), and that the wishful thinking involved in the belief in a happier hereafter is manifest.[8] Obviously, the belief in a happier hereafter is a great compensation for the unhappiness of this life and a considerable support to the tottering buttresses of one's consciousness of insecurity. It is this aspect of religious belief that has been called "an opiate of the masses," tending to make them uninterested in improving their lot on earth.

But again, the consciousness of insecurity alone is not sufficient to account for the belief in immortality. As a matter of fact there are good empirical supports for the belief in immortality, which when erroneously interpreted make a very convincing demonstration of its truth.

Among nonliterate peoples, dreams provide convincing proof the soul is capable of leaving the body and traveling to other realms. Hence, one never wakes a sleeper without giving the soul sufficient time to return to his body, for one can never tell where a sleeper's soul may wander during his slumbers. In the dream the sleeper sees himself and sometimes other persons whom he knows doing strange things in strange places. It is clear that when a person falls into a sleep from which he does not awaken, his soul has permanently departed for another abode. So death is not really cessation but translation to another sphere. Indeed, among many nonliterate peoples death is not considered to be a natural phenomenon at all. No one dies of natural causes. If it were not for the evil acts of other persons, everyone would live forever.[9] All deaths are therefore regarded as murders, which must be paid for or avenged. When a man is killed by a blow inflicted by another, the cause is plain. When he dies after a lingering or sudden illness, the cause is equally evident: It is sorcery or black magic.

Karl von den Steinen, the great German ethnologist, tells how when questioning a Bakairi Indian of Brazil as to the language of his tribe, he gave the sentence "Every man must die" to be translated into the Indian's language. The Indian greeted his request with a prolonged silence. Von den Steinen, somewhat puzzled, soon learned that the reason for this was that the Indian had no conception of the necessity of death. The cause of death is always some other person. If there were only good men in the world, said one Indian, there would be neither sickness nor death.[10] And so it is for many other peoples.[11] So that death really produces no genuine break in the continuity of life. This idea is thoroughly well supported by the experience of dreams, in which one not only sees oneself and other living persons whom one knows and some persons whom one does not know, but one also sees those who have departed. Clearly, in different translations, life goes on forever, and man is, indeed, immortal.

The denial of death as a natural phenomenon is in itself an interesting aspect of human nature, with the closest possible bearing upon our present discussion. Death is a reality that human beings pulsing with life cannot face with equanimity. Hence, what is more simple than to deny it as a reality? Why should the life of man have definite limits in time and space? Why should there be a term to his existence? Is there such a period to the lives of animals and plants? In such a state of mind men are likely to say clearly not. The grape may wither upon the vine, the petal fall from the flower and the leaf from the twig. But do they not reappear with predictable regularity, as bright and as blooming as ever? And so it is with animals. They wax and wane, just as plants do, with the seasons. It is evident to sense that all living things are constantly renewed—renewed at the springs of eternal life.

Corporeally all things may for a time pass, but spiritually there can be no doubt of their renewal, their constancy, and their continuity.

All this is beautifully exemplified by the Aivilik Eskimos of the Canadian Arctic, studied by Professor Edmund Carpenter:

> Cessation of the heart beat [for the Aivilik] remains but part of the cycle of life and death where, sooner or later, the body disappears as an entity, and the soul re-enters the cycle. The why of all this does not concern the Aivilik; they claim no transcendent ability to understand it.
>
> They merely assert that death is not an end, but a beginning—a beginning of a new phase in a never-ending cycle. They meet the problems of death by denying the problem itself. I suspect they fear, in the secret depths of their hearts, the finality of death, and that their philosophy is more denial of a reality emotionally felt than a conviction carrying full belief. Nevertheless, they maintain that they can run all risks, squander their lives, and scatter their possessions, because they are immortal. They know that there is life beyond death, beyond the corruption of the body—beyond every evidence of the disappearance of the body scattered amidst nature and the seasons.
>
> For life, they say, is superior to time. It cannot vanish, because death, like birth, is an event in time, and life is above time. This vivid belief—even if it remains unformulated, a silent assumption—is the very essence of Aivilik philosophy. It is a conviction so strong and so unshakable as to deny and defy the fact of death. Death is never an inevitability, obedient to natural laws. It is the work of a witch or deity and hence dependent upon individual and fortuitous causes. A concept of death as something that conforms to unalterable natural laws, the Aivilik never recognize. Nor do they recognize it as an ultimate end, as the

final stop in the journey of life. The entire concept of a man as mortal, by his nature and essence, is alien to them. Just as deities and angels are not imprisoned in time, so human life knows no temporal walls.

The Aivilik feel that death is not a hard, unbearable fact. It is like sleep; in both cases the body reawakens. When confronting death, they clearly reveal this feeling. If they cannot cast derision upon the supercession of breath, they meet it not with anything that can ordinarily be called fear, certainly not with any kind of hope. They are exasperated. They are, in the full sense of both words, desperately angry. For death, the destruction of life, is not so much a thing to be feared as it is first of all a thing incomprehensible, impossible, an offense, a scandal. Not-to-be is nonsense for the Aivilik. This is so true that though they meet death at every turn, although they see their relatives die, although they attend their burial, still the most difficult thing for them to believe in is death. They regard it only as an episode, an episode on the road of the immortal life of man.[12]

Such beliefs considered in the context of the general system of beliefs of nonliterate cultures are easily understandable and, in fact, inevitable. Anyone familiar with the creation myths of nonliterate peoples will recall the unity with which all life is regarded and the means by which it is constantly maintained.[13] Summarizing these myths into a typical expression, we may say that they take the following form: All life as we know it today was created by a creator. He created all living things out of the same original material or he breathed life into an originally inanimate material, and in virtue of this fact, every living thing is related to every other living thing; some are more closely related (totemism) than others, but all are related. Life is indestructible and inexhaustible. Though animals may be killed and eaten, and men may depart from

their corporeal haunts, their souls—the essential vital principle—live on forever.

As Professor Ernst Cassirer points out:

> In a certain sense the whole of mythical thought may be
> interpreted as a constant and obstinate negation of the phe-
> nomenon of death. By virtue of this conviction of the un-
> broken unity and continuity of life myth has to clear away
> this phenomenon. Primitive religion is perhaps the strongest
> and most energetic affirmation of life that we find in human
> culture.[14]

It seems to be no more complex than this: Death, because
it is not desired, is interpreted away, and life, because it is
desired, is interpreted into eternal being, and hence the belief
in immortality. All other considerations, though pertinent,
seem secondary to this. For the member of a nonliterate
culture immortality is a fact of nature, a belief by demonstration. The premises upon which the belief is based appear
to be quite sound, and there is no one to question them. Since
a fact is the consensus of opinion of those who should know,
it will be readily understood that the belief in immortality
is likely to constitute one of the most strongly entrenched of
all the beliefs held by the members of a nonliterate society.

To the question why do men believe in immortality, or,
at least, why do men in nonliterate societies believe in immortality, we may say: The belief in immortality is man's
answer to the challenge of death, his answer to the insecurities
and unhappiness of this life on earth. So believing, men can
indeed find life more tolerable upon earth than they might
otherwise find it, and this appears to be the principal function of the belief in immortality. "Say, tell me now," begins
an Aivilik death chant, "was life so nice on earth?"

It was the great German chancellor Bismarck, not a non-literate hunter, who said, "Without the hope of an afterlife this life is not even worth the effort of getting dressed in the morning."

A fact possibly of some relevance here is that up to the fifth decade of the nineteenth century the average age at death of man, throughout his long history, was thirty-three years.[15] This is equivalent to about one human generation. Life must seem quite brief to those who see it cut short so early and so often. Or is it that thirty-three years seem brief to us, who, on the average, live more than twice as long? I mention this fact in passing, for what it is worth. To those of us who manage to reach the invidious distinction of three score and ten, life seems short enough. It would seem that it would appear far shorter to men living in small communities in which early death was so frequent an occurrence. In early communities of men this fact may have contributed to the development of the idea of immortality.

What now of the belief in immortality in more sophisticated societies, in which life is so much more enduring?

THE BELIEF IN IMMORTALITY
IN LITERATE SOCIETIES

Professor Lyman Bryson has recently remarked that scientists willingly give over any wish to speak of souls.[16] But insofar as a scientist may venture to define it, he considers the soul to be the conative aspect of the mind, the same thing as the will. It is difficult to see any other meaning for the soul than the self, as Professor Bryson also realized.[17] The theologian's conception of the soul is very different. Most writers on the subject are content to say that neither the existence of the soul nor the reality of immortality can be disproved. For that matter, until recently, nor could the statement that the back of the moon is made of green cheese. As Charles S. Peirce remarked, most, if not all, reasoning on vitally important topics consists in finding reasons for what the heart desires. In any discussion of what contemporary men believe concerning the soul we must be careful not to confuse cordal with cerebral thinking.

With respect to immortality many men in the Western world today are in the position of the church warden, who when button-holed by F. W. H. Myers (one of the founders of the Society for Psychical Research) and asked what he thought would happen to him after death, after vainly trying to evade the question, burst out with "Well, I suppose I shall enter into everlasting bliss, but I do wish you would not talk about such depressing subjects." The thought was much earlier expressed by Achilles' shadow:

> I had rather live
> The servile hind for hire, and eat the bread
> Of some man scantily himself sustain'd,
> Than sov'reign empire hold over all the shades.

Thinking about the future life entails thinking about death, and *that* is distinctly an unpleasant subject, any thought of which is better repressed. Professor F. C. S. Schiller has suggested that this explains why men have not seriously encouraged inquiries into the problem of the future life. For of the "metaphysical trinity," God, freedom of the will, and immortality, the last is the only one susceptible of scientific examination and upon which science may have something vital to say. Professor Herbert Dingle puts the matter thus:

> Can common experiences, of a kind similar to those which we used to regard as characteristic of Mr. A, come to us

after the death of Mr. A? Such experiences do not normally come, but that may be because we have not established the right conditions. Psychical research, from this point of view, may therefore be a perfectly legitimate scientific procedure, although it does not follow that it is always conducted on scientific lines.

And Professor Dingle adds:

Certainly, since its findings are estimated so variously by scientific men, it cannot be said that Science has at present any definite pronouncement to make on the subject. In any case, it should be noticed that while this kind of research may conceivably establish the reality of survival, it can never give a definitive answer in the negative.[18]

In spite of all claims to the contrary there has not been a single authenticated case of communication between the dead and the living.[19] If mind and body are one it is difficult to see how there could be such communication. As J. B. S. Haldane says:

No sort of atom is peculiar to life, nor is there any evidence that anything leaves the body at death. A certain pattern of chemical events comes to an end, but there is no suggestion that vital spirits escape. . . . There is nothing to suggest that any peculiar form of energy characterizes life. The balance sheet between the energy available from food and oxygen and that put out in various ways is remarkably accurate. This is notably so in man, where it might have been expected that energy would have been converted into metaphysical forms (e.g., will or thought) or derived from metaphysical sources.[20]

It has been argued by some that the proof of the existence of life after death does not depend upon the demonstration that those who have died can communicate with the living. That may be so, but if there is any other way of demonstrating the truth of this kind of immortality, I, at least, do not know of it.

In an official Catholic source, *A Catholic Dictionary*, I find immortality defined as

> that attribute in virtue of which a being is free from death. A being is incorruptible if it does not contain within itself a principle of dissolution; it is indestructible if it can resist every external power tending to destroy or annihilate it. If the indestructible and incorruptible being is endowed with life it is called immortal. Annihilation is always possible to God by the mere withdrawal of his conserving act.[21]

Declarative statements prove nothing, but in this definition there are some demonstrative statements, and with these a scientist can deal. A scientist can show that every living thing contains within itself a principle of dissolution, and this is the principle of entropy. The principle of entropy states that energy is constantly becoming unavailable for use and that when this principle reaches its limit within the organism, the organism simply ceases to function for want of energy, because it has lost the energy necessary to keep it functioning. The organism is destroyed because it is unable to resist the external powers tending to destroy it.

In the same *Dictionary* the immortality of the soul is "proven" by a number of declarative statements and some arguments. It would take more time than I have at my disposal to examine all these statements and arguments here; most of them seem to me assumptive and circular and prove nothing more than their author's desire to prove the immortality of the soul. But apart from purely theological arguments the author of the article goes on to say "Other arguments to establish that the soul does not perish at death can be drawn (1) from the desire of perfect happiness which is unattainable in this life, and (2) from the universal judgment of mankind in the belief of a future life, a judgment which cannot lead man into error since it springs from man's rational nature."[22]

"From the desire of perfect happiness which is unattainable in this life," as I believe we have already seen, the belief in the immortality of the soul may grow, but it would be difficult to see that such a desire proves anything other than a desire for "perfect happiness," which the desirer may wish to believe is attainable in some other life. Happiness is a condition or state highly valued by human beings, and if hopes and dreams of future happiness can compensate for the lack of it in the present, the present may become more bearable, and we may the more readily endure what we are called upon to suffer.

> The miserable have no other medicine
> But only hope.

But all this is in the realm of the psychodynamics of belief and has nothing whatever to do with the proof of the existence of either a soul or its immortality. I have already indicated on what the nature of the desire for immortality may be based. The desire for or the belief in immortality is not a basic need, and the fact is that there have been and continue to be innumerable individuals who have never believed in or desired immortality. The belief in immortality, as we shall see, is a socially emergent need, a derived need, at most.

As for the statement that a proof of the fact that the soul does not perish is to be found in "the universal judgment of mankind in the belief of a future life," it may be said that if truth is to be decided by a show of hands, we leave the realm of science and enter that of the voting booth. The strength with which human beings cling to their most cherished beliefs is usually in inverse proportion to the demonstrable facts upon which they are based. Judgment originally meant critical evaluation. The universal judgment of mankind concerning immortality has hardly been that, at least no anthropologist could agree that it has been anything resembling what a scientist understands by critical evaluation. But, says the writer in the *Dictionary*, this is "a judgment that cannot lead man into error since it springs from man's rational nature."

I am not going to be so naive as to suppose that I understand what the writer means by "rational nature," but as a student of human nature I find that man's nature is wholly acquired. The potentialities he possesses for developing as a rational creature remain quite undeveloped in the absence of the necessary stimulation. That stimulation is the social interaction with other human beings in a particular cultural context, and it is according to the training the growing human being receives that his rational nature will develop. That training may be such as to render him quite unfit for making critical evaluations on any issue of a fundamental nature. What the training of most human beings does for them is to enable them to make evaluations of whatever they are called upon to evaluate in terms of the training they have received. The training in the scientific evaluation of evidence seems to me the only one that fits man for making judgments that are as nearly as possible dispassionate and objective. A very small minority of mankind has ever received such training, and it is a notable fact that it is among this class of men that there has appeared the largest proportion of agnostics and disbelievers with respect to immortality. The rest of mankind, it seems to me, for the most part has not been trained to think soundly. Man's mind is cut according to the cloth that is available, custom made, tailored according to the requirements of the cultural milieu into which he has been born, his rational nature is just that. Man's emotional or rational needs call into being abstractions that have no existence outside his own being. He calls those abstractions into being according to the kingdom that is within him, and the kingdom that is within him is determined by the cultural organization of his innate potentialities and not by any inherited "essence . . . as a principle of action," which the *Catholic Dictionary* tells me that nature is.

It is to be feared that the theological interpretations of the nature of the immortality of the soul and the proof of its existence are, from the viewpoint of the scientist, quite demonstrably unsound. It is here that I differ with some scientists and philosophers who have maintained that the scientist can have nothing to say about the theological conception of immortality. I think that not only can the scientist have something to say upon that subject but that he should also say it. "In the long run," says Freud, "nothing can withstand reason and experience. . . . We believe that it is possible for scientific work to discover something about the reality of the world through which we can increase our power and according to which we can regulate our life. . . . Science is no illusion. . . . It would be an illusion to suppose that we could get anywhere else what it cannot give us."[23]

With Freud I believe it is possible to teach men how to live more effectively and more efficiently than any religion has yet done. Humanity usually achieves its truths through a long succession of errors, fruitful errors. Has the belief in immortality been a valuable fiction, a fruitful error? We shall attempt an answer to this question in our next chapter.

With Ernest Renan (1823–92) I believe that

> the aim of humanity is not repose; it is intellectual and moral perfection. How can people talk of repose, I should like to know, when they have the infinite to traverse and the perfect to reach? Humanity will only repose when it has reached the perfect. It would be too strange if a few profane persons could, from mercenary motives or personal interest, arrest the progress of the mind, the true religious progress. The most dangerous state of humanity would be that in which the majority, finding itself quite at ease and not wishing to be disturbed, should retain its repose at the cost of thought and of an oppressed minority. . . .[24]
>
> The end of humanity, and therefore the aim which political conduct should keep before it, is to realize the highest human culture possible, that is to say the most perfect religion, by science, philosophy, art and morality: in a word by all the means of attaining the ideal which are in the nature of man.[25]

"To realize the highest human culture possible, that is to say the most perfect religion," in freedom to pursue his inquiries is a desirable end that man may yet achieve. If and when he does so, he will not have dispensed with the belief in immortality, but transformed it into a nobler form than men have yet given it: A form from which the supernatural and the supernormal elements shall have been removed and the maintenance of the principle of the eternal goodness of man installed in its stead.

I do not foresee an age when man shall be without religion. I do foresee a time when men will bring the gods

down from the heavens and naturalize them among themselves on earth, *not* as supernatural personifications of their
own projections, but as the symbols of those noble ideals that
make for the perfection of human character and personality,
the attainable ideals that lead to mental and moral health, inner
harmony, creativeness, and peace and good will. A state in
which it will be unnecessary to say that a man's grasp should
be beyond his reach or what's a heaven for, in which a man's
grasp will be educated to function within his reach and heaven
will be on earth and men will endure "Their going hence,
even as their coming hither."

Ripeness is all.

NOTES

[1] For further details see Effie Bendann, *Death Customs, An Ana-
lytical Study of Burial Rites* (New York: Knopf, 1930).

[2] In Morris Jastrow, *The Religion of Babylonia and Assyria*
(Boston, 1898), p. 519.

[3] Sir Thomas Browne, *Hydriotaphia or Urne Buriall*, Ch. 4 (London, 1658).

[4] Sir James Frazer, *The Belief in Immortality*, Vol. 1 (London:
Macmillan, 1913), p. 468.

[5] Bronislaw Malinowski, *A Scientific Theory of Culture* (Chapel
Hill: University of North Carolina Press, 1944), p. 174.

[6] Abraham Edel, "Context and Content in the Theory of Ideas,"
in *Philosophy for the Future*, ed. by R. W. Sellars, V. J. McGill, and
M. Farber (New York: Macmillan, 1949), p. 444.

[7] The id, the territory of the mind, in the Freudian sense, which
is the source of instinctual energies seeking discharge, and altogether
unconscious and unorganized.

[8] J. C. Flügel, *Man, Morals and Society* (New York: International Universities Press, 1945), p. 225.

[9] Interestingly enough, I have encountered this belief in a seven-
year-old American boy, who was convinced that no one would ever

die if they were not shot. Passing by a cemetery he remarked, "There lie all the people who have been shot. Daddy, when am I going to be shot?" Piecing together what he had heard on the radio and seen in movies and comics, he reasoned that all people died of bullets. At nine years of age this same boy believed so intensely in the reality of dreams that when his older sister asked for enlightenment concerning a detail of the dream he was narrating he rebuked her with the remark, "Oh don't be silly. You ought to know, you were in the dream." A writer in *Time* (November 12, 1965, p. 52) remarks, "Children of the TV generation are such strangers to natural death that on hearing that Grandfather is dead, they have been known to ask: 'Who shot him?' "

[10] Karl von den Steinen, *Unter den Naturvölkern Zentral-Brasiliens* (Berlin, 1894), pp. 344, 348.

[11] The evidence is summarized in Sir James Frazer, *op. cit.*

[12] Edmund Carpenter, "Eternal Life," *Explorations,* Vol. 2 (University of Toronto, 1954), pp. 59–65.

[13] For an interesting discussion of these see Sir James Frazer, *Creation and Evolution in Primitive Cosmogonies* (New York: Macmillan, 1935).

[14] Ernst Cassirer, *An Essay on Man* (New Haven: Yale University Press, 1944), p. 84.

[15] See M. F. Ashley Montagu, *An Introduction to Physical Anthropology,* ed. (Springfield, Ill.: Charles C. Thomas, 1961), p. 545.

[16] Lyman Bryson, *Science and Freedom* (New York: Columbia University Press, 1947), p. 99.

[17] *Ibid.,* p. 106.

[18] Herbert Dingle, *Science and Human Experience* (New York: Macmillan, 1932), p. 133.

[19] For a discussion of the whole subject from the standpoint of the student of psychical research, see G. N. M. Tyrrel's interesting book, *The Personality of Man* (West Drayton, Middlesex: Penguin Books, 1948).

[20] J. B. S. Haldane, "Interaction of Physics, Chemistry, and Biology," in *Philosophy for the Future* (New York: Macmillan, 1949), pp. 204, 205.

[21] *A Catholic Dictionary,* ed. by Donald Attwater (New York: Macmillan, 1941), p. 261.

[22] *Ibid.,* p. 261.

[23] Sigmund Freud, *The Future of an Illusion* (London: Hogarth Press, 1928), pp. 94, 95, 98.

[24] Ernest Renan, *The Future of Science* (London: Chapman and Hall, 1891), p. 403.

[25] *Ibid.*, p. 342.

CHAPTER 3

Immortality and Ethics

O joy! that in our embers
Is something that doth live,
That Nature yet remembers
What was so fugitive!
—William Wordsworth,
Ode on Intimations of Immortality

ETHICS IS the department of human behavior relating to morals or the principles of human duty. The word is derived from the Greek and means manners, the manners of people, their way of life. In its more academic sense it is usually understood as the study of wisdom in conduct, of right conduct. In this chapter I shall consider the relation of the belief in immortality to the conduct of men. In the past the belief in immortality has influenced men for both good and evil. Here we shall ask ourselves whether there is any kind of immortality that the rigorous thinker can accept, and we shall inquire to what extent any such belief can contribute to wisdom and the good life.

Where life, as Hobbes put it, is nasty, brutish, and short, it is obvious that the belief in immortality would make life more bearable on earth. The assurance in this life of a happier life in another world in reincarnated form provides an immediate and more or less continuous gratification in the knowledge that happiness is certain. Complete immediate happiness is not the lot of man on earth; its postponement by the gods or fates is in the interest of greater long-term satisfactions. Adults have taught children that they must forgo certain immediate pleasures in order to reap greater long-term advantages, and this is a pattern of behavior familiar to most human beings before they have grown very old in childhood. Hence the belief in happiness accruing to one in another world in proportion to one's obedience in this world is akin to the parental promise of rewards to come conditional upon good behavior now. I am here suggesting that just as men frequently project the image of their parents upon the background of the world in which they create their gods and often call their gods "Great Father," "All Protecting" or "All Powerful Father," or "Great Mother" or "All Protecting Mother," and the like, so men tend to organize themselves in relation to the world according to the configuration of rewards and punishments in which they have been conditioned during childhood.[1] In this sense heaven stands for the ideal of goodness, it is a projection of the conception of goodness, while hell is a projection of evil, of conscience, of what the psychoanalyst calls the super-ego. Hamlet describes the condition in his famous soliloquy:

> who would fardels bear,
> To grunt and sweat under a weary life,
> But that the dread of something after death,—
> The undiscover'd country, from whose bourn
> No traveller returns,—puzzles the will,
> And makes us rather bear those ills we have

Than fly to others that we know not of?
Thus conscience does make cowards of us all;
And thus the native hue of resolution
Is sicklied o'er with the pale cast of thought;
And enterprises of great pith and moment,
With this regard, their currents turn awry,
And lose the name of action.

The culture and personality school of anthropologists
has made a number of valuable contributions to this field, but
research on the relation of child-rearing processes to the kinds
of belief in immortality that prevail in human societies has
not been conducted on any significant scale. For the cultures
of the Western world, however, we do have some knowledge
of the nature of child-rearing processes and the kinds of
belief in immortality that prevail in them. In these cultures
the belief in heaven and hell and the belief in immortality are
general; life after death, it is believed, is spent in the one or
the other according to the life the individual has led on earth.
In other words, whether one's existence will be spent after
death in heaven or in hell is conditional upon one's behavior
on earth. And this, I think we may readily see, constitutes
something of a mirror of the socialization process prevailing
over a large part of the Western world that children are made
to undergo. The love of the parents for the children is, in the
process of socialization or discipline, made conditional upon
the children's behaving in certain required ways, which are
called "good." If the children are good they will be loved,
if they are not good they will be punished.[2] If they are good,
they will enjoy, as it were, heaven on earth; if they are not
good, they will suffer, as it were, hell on earth. Gradually
children learn that this process is extended to their existence
in the next world, and as adults they believe that the good

alone enter heaven and the evil go to hell. Heaven is a reward for good behavior on earth, hell or purgatory the punishment for evil behavior on earth.

Thus, we may perceive that in origin, as a projection of the pattern of childhood discipline, the belief in immortality becomes a social discipline for the regulation of human behavior. In addition to the immediate rewards and punishments that follow upon one's conduct on earth and exercise a regulative effect upon one's behavior, the belief in immortality has added an even stronger regulative effect upon the conduct of men. The desire for eternal happiness and the fear of eternal punishment have been among the strongest factors in encouraging men to adhere to whatever their society conceived to be the good life. With the unready and premature jettisoning of such beliefs in certain parts of the Western world there has gone a breakdown in the moral fiber of large numbers of persons who would not otherwise have been left spiritually rudderless in a world at sea. Listen to these prophetic words of Ernest Renan, from the preface to his great book *The Future of Science*, written in 1848 but not published till 1890:

If through the constant labor of the nineteenth century the knowledge of facts has considerably increased, the destiny of mankind has on the other hand become more obscure than ever. The serious thing is that we fail to perceive a means of providing humanity in the future with a catechism that will be acceptable henceforth, except on the condition of returning to a state of credulity. Hence, it is possible that the ruin of idealistic beliefs may be fated to follow hard upon the ruin of supernatural beliefs and that the real abasement of the morality of humanity will date from the day it has seen the reality of things. Chimeras have succeeded in obtaining from the good gorilla an astonishing moral effort; do away with the chimeras and part of the factitious energy they aroused will disappear. Even glory as a motive power implies in some respects immortality, the fruit of it generally coming only after death. Suppress the alcohol on which the workman has hitherto relied for his strength, but you must not ask him for the same amount of work.[3]

The image-breakers of the nineteenth century threw out too much of the bathtub in their efforts to hold on to the baby, and the new model with which they have supplied him gives him a highly polished but too slippery surface upon which either to stand or rise.

Renan believed thoroughly in the future of science and did not believe in supporting men in false beliefs. He did, however, believe that before removing the crutches from anyone recovering from a crippling sickness one should make perfectly sure that he is strong enough to stand on his feet. This is precisely what we have failed to do with twentieth-century man recovering from the turmoil of the nineteenth century. Our scientific gadgetry has been encouraged to outrun our moral effort. Our high-powered civilization is geared to low ethics.[4] Having toppled the gods of our fathers from their pedestals, we now worship at other shrines the idols of science and of the marketplace. As a direct and inevitable consequence we have entered an age of immorality, and we have lived to see at least one great nation's government enthrone immorality as a political doctrine for all its people to practice. We have lived to see men abandon all morality in the name of morality and in the name of the state torture and murder millions of human beings while untold suffering was deliberately and brutally inflicted upon millions of others. We have lived to witness the virtues men have over the millennia so dearly learned trampled roughshod under-

foot and goodness redefined as weakness. We have beheld
men who have been brought up in a so-called Christian world
ready to trade with what served them for a conscience and
deal with Nazis and fascists on their own terms.

If you deny men their illusions, what will they live by?
Reality? For most men reality is a poor substitute for make-
believe. It is a challenge too hard for them to accept. Hence,
the prevalence of myth. Before destroying the illusions men
live by, one must be careful to see that they are replaced by
something at least as satisfying.

The fear of death is not, as it has sometimes been described, an elemental one. Socrates died well and in good
cheer. Jesus died in agony, with his deep human cry of
desertion and loneliness. The Greeks considered that the body
constituted a limitation and impediment to the soul, a prison-
house from which death brought to the soul release into a
fuller existence. Christianity, on the other hand, reflecting
the mode of Christ's death, based its doctrine of immortality
on the resurrection of the body, the reunion of the body with
the soul.

The being and nothingness, the meaningless death at the
end of a meaningless life, offered by the existentialists, is a
bleak and unappealing doctrine. It is in utter opposition to
that healthy and even joyful life by which men can learn
to live were they but afforded the opportunity of the discipline and freedom to do so.

There is a tragic element to life, which is an indissoluble
part of it. Death is unpardonable, bereavement beyond the
reach of consolation, and there is little hope this side of
despair. Time is the enemy and wounds us with its days, and
soon enough, with its scythe, will mow us all down. The
grinning skeleton is present at the revels of Everyman, and
the Pale Horse and Rider of the Apocalypse will cut down

millions of innocents before their time. Death may be wooed or held in contempt, but it cannot be outwitted. We must all, therefore, learn to live with it.

Millions of men and women live for the moment and have learned to live for the future only insofar as the moment matters, for the last moment is for them the end in both senses of the word. And this brings us to an eternally important truth: Those who have not learned how to die have not learned how to live. This, it would appear, is one of the ends the belief in immortality is designed to secure. To learn that in order to live well, one must die well. If one believes that one doesn't have to die well, there seems no particular point to living well—and by well is meant according to one's conscience or the canons of moral goodness prevailing in one's society—if there appear to be more genuinely realistic and immediate satisfactions in living for the moment by any means one finds pleasurable. Under such conditions of belief the postponement of certain immediate gratifications appears unreasonable and otiose.

In this life we may linger and suffer, but while there is hope, the expectation, of a richer life beyond, it matters not how strait the gate, for of the promised future life one is certain, and certain that one will live in it forever.

> Whether we be young or old,
> Our destiny, our being's heart and home,
> Is with infinitude, and only there;
> With hope it is, hope that can never die,
> Effort, and expectation, and desire,
> And something evermore about to be.[5]

It should be clear that the belief in immortality constitutes a denial of death. As Freud has pointed out, "Negation of reality is a transition phase between ignoring and accepting reality; the alien and therefore hostile outer world becomes capable of entering consciousness, in spite of 'pain,' when it is supplied with the minus prefix of negation, *i.e.*, when it is denied."[6] Sylvia Anthony, in her remarkable study *The Child's Discovery of Death,* found that in the children she studied in England a certain amount of anxiety about death was normal. When the idea of death first comes into association with the idea of self, a normal critical anxiety is likely to develop, and this tends to be reduced by the development of a belief, in one form or another, in immortality. I have already mentioned that this is likely to be patterned on the type of discipline the child has undergone at the hands of its parents. Now, observe what happens during the socialization process. Miss Anthony quotes a number of cases of which the following is typical. This account refers to Richard, aged five years:

> Once or twice lately, at bath-time, R. has begun to get whimpering and miserable about dying. Yesterday he played with the possibility of never dying, living to a thousand, etc., as he swam up and down in his bath. But to-day:
>
> R.: I might be alone when I die. Will you be with me? . . . But I don't want to be dead, ever; I don't want to die.
>
> This raised difficulties, because a day or two before his trouble had seemed that he did not know how to die; he seemed to be worried mainly about his inefficiency, and M. had told him he need not worry, because she would die first, and he could see what it was like—this seemed to satisfy him at the time. However, M. now assured him that she would be with him when he died. Then:
>
> M.: But you won't die for a long time, Richard. You won't die till after you understand about it.

At this a smile gradually broke over his very serious, unhappy face, and he said: That's all right. I've been worried, and now I can get happy. (He jumped about on the bathmat, and sang a little with relief.)

A few minutes later:

R.: I wish I could dream in the day-time.

M.: What would you like to dream about?

R.: About going shopping and buying things.[7]

The reaction of the mother is typically interesting, as is the denial by the child of something it had already conceived. Miss Anthony found that the mothers assured the children that they would not die, for as she says, the question of postponement until there was understanding is for the child practically equivalent to an assurance of immortality. Many mothers, acting, it would seem, on an empathic understanding of the child's needs, mythologize the idea of death for them. "You go far, far away, and live happily ever after," or "You become whatever you'd like to be," and so on. It is in such terms that certain ideas are most easily reconciled with the child's own inner needs. The need to deny certain perceived realities appears to be a normal stage in the acceptance of reality. In going along with the child, in helping him at his stage of development to negate reality, the mother assists the child to accept reality when he is ready for it. Refusal to assist in this way causes the child to escape its anxiety in a manner less conformable with its stage of mental development and its individual personality. "Thus," remarks Miss Anthony, "it seems that the child may weave for himself, and need agreement to help him weave and maintain, a belief in personal immortality. That the self will die is the reality which is only to be entertained when supplied with the minus prefix of negation."[8]

And how may death further be continued to be denied? How may one continue to live forever on earth? These are questions Samuel Butler (1835–1902) dealt with in a famous chapter of *Erewhon Revisited*, and called the physics of vicarious existence. But we run a little ahead of ourselves here and will return to the answer to these questions after we have devoted a few more words to the ethical implications of the belief in immortality.

The belief in immortality is the prototypic act of faith, and as such it forms the foundation of man's belief in spirits, and, as Tylor stated many years ago, the belief in spirits is religion. The belief in immortality, then, stands at the very base of man's religious beliefs. There are some possible exceptions to this statement, as early Confucianism, for example. But then, by definition Confucianism was originally not a religion but a philosophic way of life. In general, the statement appears to be true. The socially cohesive functions religion performs for men living in human societies owe much to the conception of immortality that prevails in them. It is interesting to find that in the East and in the Orient, in the cultures in which children appear to be brought up on the whole permissively, the belief in immortality should take a form so different from that which prevails in the cultures of the West. Thus, Professor F. C. S. Northrop tells us that:

in Buddhism as in Taoism and Confucianism, and also . . . in Hinduism, there is no immortality of the full, *differentiated*, immediately apprehended, or postulationally conceived, personality. Only the immediately apprehended aesthetic field component which is common to all persons and all aesthetic things is immortal.

This conclusion has its basis in the fact that all differentiated, determinate things are transitory. Any immediately apprehended, specifically sensed differentiation of the aesthetic continuum, such as a specific blue characterizing a local, limited portion of the aesthetic manifold, is temporal and temporary. It arises out of the undifferentiated continuum and fades back into it again. Thus the Buddhist arrives at his basic thesis that all determinate things, even the determinate portion of the personality, that which differentiates one person from another, is mortal and transitory.[9]

Do Eastern parents give their children a greater sense of security than do Western parents and thus render it unnecessary to deny the reality of death? This is a problem that remains to be investigated, but what I wish to draw attention to here is the further remark of Professor Northrop, continuing from where we last broke off:

In fact, one of the most insistent contentions of the Buddhist, and of the Oriental sages generally, is that the emphasis on the immortality of the determinate portion of the self is not merely a conclusion to which the immediately apprehended facts of experience give the lie, but also a positive source of selfishness. Thus the Oriental sage is continuously insisting that one must become self-less. Put more positively, what he is saying is that the self is composed of two components, one a determinate, differentiated, unique element, distinguishing one person from any other person; the other the all-embracing, aesthetically immediate, and emotionally moving compassionate indeterminate, and hence indescribable, field component. The former is temporary, transitory, and not immortal; furthermore, the cherishing of it, the desire for its immortality, is a source of suffering, selfishness and evil. The part of the self which is not transitory and immortal is the aesthetic field component of the self. Because it is identical not merely in all persons but in all aesthetic objects throughout the entire cosmos, the cherishing of it, instead of making men selfish, gives them a compassionate fellow-feeling for all creatures. The way to secure peace of mind and religious contentment is, according to the Buddhist, not to go on, as the Western Christian does, optimistically assuming and cherishing the immortality of the complete, differentiated, determinate, unique personality. Such a procedure is false to the immediately apprehended fact that all differentiations, all determinate things in the complex, differentiated aesthetic continuum, are transitory. At this point the Buddhist—and the Oriental generally—is as realistic as the most hard-boiled Western materialist or contemporary relativistic naturalist.[10]

I have quoted this account of the Oriental conception of immortality to show how different it is from that which has most generally prevailed in the Western world, but most of all to show how the particular kind of conception of immortality in which a people believes will influence the character of its religious beliefs and the attitudes of the believers to their fellow men.

Surveying the history of man, I think we can see that the belief in immortality has not been an unmitigated good, though I believe there can be little doubt that on the whole the belief has worked for good rather than otherwise. At the same time it remains true that the belief in immortality has often caused men to take too careless a view of life, of the lives of others as well as of their own.[11] The many men who have thrown away their lives under the impression that by so doing they would the more readily enter upon eternal life in heaven, and millions of others in their concentration upon heavenly bliss, have paid too little attention to the manner in which it could be earned on earth, as our Oriental sages have penetratingly observed. But if the belief in immortality has made some men careless of their lives and others lazy, it has

caused innumerable others to live their lives more fully and
with greater security and serenity than they would otherwise,
under their particular conditions of life, have been able to do.
As Malinowski has pointed out, the belief in immortality
secures a bond of union between the living and the dead,
which is a fact of immense importance for the continuity of
culture and for the safe keeping of tradition.[12]

The belief in immortality serves to integrate the personality and to secure the cohesion of the social fabric, and
since all men have a need to be recognized and appreciated,
the consciousness that they will be noticed on earth sufficiently to be rewarded with everlasting life in the hereafter
is a valued accretion to their positive self-feeling. Because the
belief in immortality encourages and supports men in their
postponement of certain gratifications it has played a major
role in maintaining social equilibrium. The ethical standards
that are everywhere associated with the belief in immortality
have, in addition, further contributed to the stabilizing of the
relations between men. On the whole, the belief in immortality has served to increase the respect for and understanding
of life as well as of death and has helped significantly to
reduce an anxiety among men that might otherwise have
been seriously socially disruptive. In short, the belief in immortality has, on the whole, served to make men better than
they would otherwise have been.

A FAITH IN IMMORTALITY FOR MODERN MAN

In the remaining portion of this chapter I wish to deal with a
conception of immortality in which all men can believe—a
faith in immortality for modern men. There is nothing new
in this conception of immortality; it is at least as old as Buddhism, and it is one in which innumerable men believe at the

present time. It has been frequently discussed by poets, philosophers, publicists, and scientists, indeed, by many classes
of thinkers, perhaps most effectively by Samuel Butler in his
Erewhon Revisited (1901). In chapter eleven of that work,
"President Gurgoyle's Pamphlet on the Physics of Vicarious
Existence," Butler brilliantly presents the conception of immortality I have in mind here, and I should like to quote the
relevant passages:

> Dr. Gurgoyle, however, had an equal horror, on the
> one hand, of anything involving resumption of life by the
> body when it was once dead and on the other of the view
> that life ended with the change which we call death. He did
> not, indeed, pretend that he could do much to take away
> the sting from death, nor would he do this if he could, for if
> men did not fear death unduly, they would often court it
> unduly. Death can only be belauded at the cost of belittling
> life; but he held that a reasonable assurance of fair fame after
> death is a truer consolation to the dying, a truer comfort to
> surviving friends, and a more real incentive to good conduct
> in this life, than any of the consolations or incentives falsely
> fathered upon the Sunchild. . . .
> Life, he urged, lies not in bodily organs, but in the
> power to use them, and in the use that is made of them—
> that is to say, in the work they do. As the essence of a fac-
> tory is not in the building wherein the work is done nor yet
> in the implements used in turning it out, but in the will-
> power of the master and in the goods he makes; so the true
> life of a man is in his will and work, not in his body.
> "Those," he argued, "who make the life of a man reside in
> his body, are like one who should mistake the carpenter's
> toolbox for the carpenter." . . .
> He went on to say that our will-power is not wholly
> limited to the working of its own special system of organs,
> but under certain conditions can work and be worked upon

by other will-powers like itself: so that if, for example, A's will-power has got such a hold on B's as to be able, through B, to work B's mechanism, what seems to have been B's action will in reality have been more A's than B's and this is the same real sense as though the physical action had been affected through A's own mechanical system—A, in fact, will have been living in B. The universally admitted maxim that he who does this or that by the hand of an agent does it himself, shows that the foregoing view is only a round-about way of stating what common sense treats as a matter of course.

Hence, though A's individual will-power must be held to cease when the tools it works are destroyed or out of gear, yet so long as any survivors were so possessed by it while it was still efficient, or, again, become so impressed by its operation on them through work that he has left as to act in obedience to his will-power rather than their own, A has a certain amount of *bona fide* life still remaining. His vicarious life is not affected by the dissolution of his body; and in many cases the sum total of a man's vicarious action and of its outcome exceeds to an almost infinite extent the sum total of those actions and works that were effected through the mechanism of his own physical organs. In these cases his vicarious life is more truly his life than any that he lived in his own person. . . .

This vicarious life . . . is lived by every one of us before death as well as after it, and is little less important to us than that of which we are to some extent conscious in our own persons. A man, we will say, has written a book which delights or displeases thousands of whom he knows nothing, and who know nothing of him. The book, we will suppose, has considerable, or at any rate some influence on the action of these people. Let us suppose the writer fast asleep while others are enjoying his work, and acting in consequence of it, perhaps at long distances from him. Which is his truest

life—the one he is leading in them, or that equally unconscious life residing in his own sleeping body? Can there be
a doubt that the vicarious life is the more efficient?

Or when we are waking, how powerfully does not the
life we are living in others pain or delight us? How truly
do we not recognize it as part of our own existence, and
how great an influence does not the fear of the present hell
in men's bad thoughts, and the hope of a present heaven in
their good ones, influence our own conduct? Have we not
here a true heaven and a true hell, as compared with the
efficiency of which these gross material ones so falsely en-
grafted on the Sunchild's teaching are but as the flint implements of a prehistoric race? "If a man," said the Sunchild,
"fear not man, whom he hath seen, neither will he fear God,
whom he hath not seen." . . .

It may be urged that on a man's death one of the great
factors of his life is so annihilated that no kind of true life
can be any further conceded to him. For to live is to be
influenced, as well as to influence; and when a man is dead
how can he be influenced? He can haunt, but he cannot any
more be haunted. He can come to us, but we cannot go to
him. On ceasing, therefore, to be impressionable, so great a
part of that wherein his life consisted is removed, that no
true life can be conceded him.

I do not pretend that a man is fully alive after his so-
called death as before it. He is not. All I contend for is that
a considerable amount of efficient life still remains to some
of us, and that a little life remains to all of us, after what we
commonly regard as the complete cessation of life. In answer, then, to those who have just urged that the destruction
of one of the two great factors of life destroys life altogether, I reply that the same must hold good as regards
death.

If to live is to be influenced and to influence, and if a
man cannot be held as living when he can no longer be

influenced, surely to die is to be no longer able to influence or to be influenced, and a man cannot be held dead until both these two factors of death are present. If failure of the power to be influenced vitiates life, presence of the power to influence vitiates death. And no one will deny that a man can influence for many a long year after he is vulgarly reputed dead. . . .

The Sunchild was never weary of talking to us . . . about a great poet of that nation to which it pleased him to feign that he belonged. How plainly can we not now see that his words were spoken for our learning—for the enforcement of that true view of heaven and hell on which I am feebly trying to insist? The poet's name, he said, was Shakespeare. Whilst he was alive, very few people understood his greatness; whereas now, after some three hundred years, he is deemed the greatest poet the world has ever known. "Can this man," he asked, "be said to have been truly born till many a long year after he had been reputed as truly dead? While he was in the flesh, was he more than a mere embryo growing towards birth into that life of the world to come in which he now shines so gloriously? What a small thing was that flesh and blood life, of which he was alone conscious, as compared with that fleshless life which he lives but knows not in the lives of millions, and which, had it ever fully revealed even to his imagination, we may be sure that he could not have reached?"

. . . Which, then, of this man's two lives should we deem best worth having, if we could choose one or the other, but not both? The felt or the unfelt? Who would not go cheerfully to block or stake if he knew that by doing so he could win such a life as this poet lives, though he also knew that on having won it he could know no more about it? Does not this prove that in our heart of hearts we deem an unfelt life, in the heaven of men's loving thoughts, to be better worth having than any we can reasonably hope for and still feel?

The whole chapter should be read. Speaking through his characters, Butler gives us a view of immortality to which, I believe, every man may subscribe, and one may opine that it is a viewpoint that all mankind will one day universally embrace. A great part of mankind has already gone a long way toward doing so. For twenty-five centuries the Chinese have believed in this form of immortality; the Buddhists have done so for an almost equally long period of time. They have believed in the immortality of virtue or character, in the immortality of achievement or worth, and in the immortality of the spoken or written word, or, as Hu Shih has put it, the immortality of the three "w's," worth, work, and words. But, as Hu Shih has pointed out, the conception of immortality embraced by the three "w's" is too aristocratic, too exclusive. How many people can achieve or feel that they can achieve immortality in this way? Relatively few. Furthermore, this doctrine fails to furnish a negative check on human conduct. If it is to work we need a conception of immortality to which all men can feel heir. What we need is not an aristocratic but a democratic conception of immortality, a belief in the truth that everyone is immortal in the sense that whatever men do lives on somehow, somewhere, somewhen, that there is an immortality of the evil that men do as well as of the good that they do, of the vulgar as well as of the sublime, of the ugly as well as of the beautiful, of stupidity as well as of wisdom, of selfishness as well as of service—the immortality, in short, of what one *is*. This is the religion of social immortality, the social physics of vicarious existence. Humanity is what it is because of the wisdom and the folly of our fathers, of those who have preceded us. Future humanity will similarly be what it is as a consequence of the wisdom and folly of ourselves. This men must learn to understand, and it is here that the doctrine of social immortality will be most helpful, though I am not suggesting that the reform of humanity will be brought about by the simple means of persuading all men to subscribe to such a doctrine. I am, however, suggesting that by this means alone great progress would be made in the right direction. Obviously, many other social changes will be necessary before such a belief can naturally grow in the soil of human relations. And this brings us full tilt to the question of ethics. The belief in social immortality entails a conception of human relations that makes every man dependent upon and interdependent with his fellows, his contemporaries, but also those who have mortally passed from this earth and especially those who are yet to be born. By the measure of the conception of social immortality every man is responsible for everything to everyone else, for in the moving words of John Donne (1572–1631):

> No man is an Island, entire of itself; every man is a piece of the Continent, a part of the main; if a Clod be washed away by the Sea, Europe is the less, as well as if a Promontory were; as well as if a Manor of thy friends or of thine own were; any man's death diminishes me, because I am involved in Mankind; And therefore never send to know for whom the bell tolls; it tolls for thee.

My own studies have led me to the conclusion that the work bearing on man that has been done during the past half-century points to the fact that man is born with the strongest desires for cooperation, for love, that he is born good, in the sense that were his needs adequately satisfied he would, in the encouraging environment, experience no great difficulty in developing into a good human being in the best sense of those words.[13] The good of which man is so eminently capable society should make it possible for him to realize. Toward this end I see no more effective means of bringing about the necessary changes in the minds of men than through education. There are men who believe that such changes can only be brought about by violent revolution and the overthrow of existing institutions; so only, do they believe, could the proper education be provided for the masses of mankind. On the other hand, I am convinced that the only way in which true revolutions are brought about is through education—in the minds of men.

Human relations are the most important of all the relations into which men can enter. A human being can be related to himself only insofar as he is related to other human beings. The greatest gift a man can offer to his fellows is his character, not his intentions but his actual personality in all its activities. And, as Aristotle puts it in the *Nicomachean Ethics*, "the God of man proves to be the active exercise of his soul's faculties in conformity with excellence or virtue, or if there be several human excellences or virtues, in conformity with the best and most perfect among them."[14] And, as Aristotle later adds:

> Nor ought we to obey those who enjoin that a man should have man's thoughts and a mortal the thoughts of mortality, but we ought so far as possible to achieve immortality, and do all that man may live in accordance with the highest things in him (*i.e.* the intellect); for though this be small in bulk, in power and in value it surpasses all the rest.[15]

We, too, I believe must place our faith in the power of the intellect to steer us safely toward the discovery of the true criteria by which men may best live. Some men have already made that discovery and have resolved to live as if to live and love were one in the recognition, as Whitehead has somewhere put it, that life can be cultivated, that "culture is activity of thought and receptiveness to beauty, and *humane feeling*." It is in the humane feeling that, it is to be feared, Aristotle was weak. Aristotle took an aristocratic view of life, and his works were written for aristocrats. It requires, therefore, to be pointed out that intellect without *humanitas* is cold, superior, marvelous, and at the same time the most dangerous thing in the world. In whatever ways man arrives at his beliefs, he uses his intellect to justify them and to give them an intellectual basis. Whether that basis is referred to the supernatural or the natural is beside the point here. What is to the point is that the intellect does the rationalizing, the cataloguing, the interpreting, and the analyzing. It is therefore of the first importance to see to it that that intellect is warmed by the fires of the human heart, the consciousness that the love of one's fellow men is beyond everything else the fundamental and primary quality of men, for without this love of his fellow men, man may be limitedly intelligent but he will not necessarily be humane. It is because intelligence may be used or misused for any end whatsoever—to make men members of Plato's Republic, of Mussolini's fascist state, of Hitler's Nazi Third Reich, and of Stalin's Soviet Union—that we must insist upon this prime requisite of humanity, of love of one's fellow men before all else.

We live by a pure flame within us; that flame is love. It is the source from which we draw and convey our warmth to others. It is the light that guides us in relation to our fellow men; it is the flame before which we warm the hands of life and without which we remain cold and lusterless all the days of our lives. Love is the light of the world, causing a spring of virtues where it shines. It is the task of each of us to keep that flame burning, for if we fail to do that, there is a real danger that the light will go out of the world.

As Isaac Rosenberg, who was killed on the Western front in 1918, wrote,

They only live who have not lived in vain,
For in their works their life returns again.

Ernest Renan, in his *The Future of Science*, uttered the same thought. "Immortality," he wrote, "means to labor at a lasting work."

It is through our work, through our deeds, through our influence, that we can become the instruments of something greater than ourselves. It is personal influence that determines the size of a life.

The one indestructible thing in this world is the spirit of man. It is the deeds that that spirit leads him to that live on eternally in him and in his fellow men. I know of no better evidence of this than the story of a prisoner of the Nazis. They were torturing him in order to extract from him the names of his friends. When all physical means had failed, they took a psychological approach.

"You are a hero," they said. "You have shown magnificent courage, but it will do you no good. You are here helpless in this dungeon, and here you will die. Why not spare yourself an agony of pain, for no one will ever know of your heroism."

"I will know," the prisoner replied, "and I will know that since I am no better and no worse than other men, all mankind is capable of what you choose to call my heroism."

In his admirable book, *The Nature of the Universe*, Fred Hoyle remarks:

Here we are in this wholly fantastic Universe with scarcely a clue as to whether our existence has any real significance

No wonder then that many people feel the need for some belief that gives them a sense of security, and no wonder they become very angry with people like me who say that this security is illusory.[16]

Hoyle can see no advantage in deceiving oneself. But the point is that for most human beings the belief in immortality has been not a matter of self-deception but a valuable means of reducing anxiety and making life more tolerable. The fact is, as Hoyle says, that we do live in a fantastic universe with scarcely a clue as to whether our existence has any real significance. But if this is so, then surely our only course is to say, with Nietzsche and Kierkegaard: Why you exist nobody in the world can tell you in advance; but since you do exist, try to give your existence a meaning by setting up for yourself as lofty and noble a goal as you can.[17]

In "Dover Beach" Matthew Arnold has captured the mood:

Ah love, let us be true
To one another! For the world, which seems
To lie before us like a land of dreams,
So various, so beautiful, so new,
Hath neither joy, nor love, nor light,
Nor certitude, nor peace, nor help for pain;
And we are here as on a darkling plain
Swept with confused alarms of struggle and flight
Where ignorant armies clash by night.

Is this really true? Is this ineffectual melancholy, this abandonment of all hope, this beautifully expressed description of the lot of most human beings, all that there is to be said? Is there, in fact, no joy or love or light, and is there no possibility of certitude, peace, and help for pain?

On this "darkling plain" we may already perceive that there is. Man makes his own certitudes, precisely as he makes himself.

Professor J. T. Shotwell has pointed out that there are two kinds of immortality:

> the immortality of monuments,—of things to look at and recall; and the immortality of use,—of things which surrender their identity but continue to live, things forgotten but treasured, and incorporated in the vital forces of society. Thought can achieve both kinds. It embodies itself in forms, —like epics, cathedrals and even engines,—where the endurance depends upon the nature of the stuff used, the perfection of the workmanship and the fortune of time. But it also embodies itself in use; that is, it can continue to work, enter into other thought and continue to emit its energy even when its original mold is broken up.[18]

It is the wonder of thought that it can become disembodied and influence men forever afterward. And since men's thoughts are a reflection of their souls, of themselves, their souls, in this sense, may be said to live on in their thoughts, in their deeds, in their works. And this, I believe, is the only real immortality. For myself, as a social biologist, this truth has been most beautifully expressed in the poem of that immortal woman, George Eliot:

> Oh may I join the choir invisible
> Of those immortal dead who live again
> In minds made better by their presence: live
> In deeds of daring rectitude, in scorn
> For miserable aims that end with self,
> In thoughts sublime that pierce the night like stars,
> And with their mild persistence urge man's search

To vaster issues.
          So to live is heaven:
To make undying music in the world,
Breathing as beauteous order that controls
With growing sway the growing life of man.
So we inherit that sweet purity,
For which we struggled, failed, and agonized
With widening retrospect that bred despair.
Rebellious flesh that would not be subdued,
A vicious parent shaming still its child
Poor anxious penitence, is quick dissolved;
Its discords, quenched by meeting harmonies,
Die in the large and charitable air.
And all our rarer, better, truer self,
That sobbed religiously in yearning song,
That watched to ease the burthen of the world,
Laboriously tracing what must be,
And what may yet be better—saw within
A worthier image for the sanctuary,
And shaped it forth before the multitude
Divinely human, raising worship so
To higher reverence more mixed with love—
That better self shall live till human Time
Shall fold its eyelids, and the human sky
Be gathered like a scroll within the tomb
Unread for ever.
          This is life to come,
Which martyred men have made more glorious
For us who strive to follow. May I reach
That purest heaven, be to other souls
The cup of strength in some great agony,
Enkindle generous ardour, feed pure love,
Beget the smiles that have no cruelty—
Be the sweet presence of a good diffused,
And in diffusion ever more intense.

So shall I join the choir invisible
Whose music is the gladness of the world.

NOTES

[1] After this passage was written I discovered that the idea was by no means new and that reference had already been made to it by Erich Fromm, Wilhelm Reich, and Abraham Kardiner. See Kardiner's book *The Individual and His Society* (New York: Columbia University Press, 1939), p. 76.

[2] For a discussion of the concept of "conditional love," see Margaret Mead's *And Keep Your Powder Dry* (New York: Morrow, 1942).

[3] Ernest Renan, *The Future of Science* (London: Chapman & Hall, 1891), pp. xviii–xix.

[4] I owe this remark to Professor Lee M. Brooks, "Fifty Years' Quest for Social Control," *Social Forces*, Vol. 29 (1950), p. 7.

[5] William Wordsworth, *The Prelude*, Bk. VI, ll. 603–8.

[6] Sigmund Freud, "Negation," *International Journal of Psychoanalysis*, Vol. 6 (1925), pp. 361–67.

[7] Sylvia Anthony, *The Child's Discovery of Death* (New York: Harcourt, Brace & World, 1940), p. 185.

[8] *Ibid.*, p. 186.

[9] F. C. S. Northrop, *The Meeting of East and West* (New York: Macmillan, 1946), pp. 352–53.

[10] *Ibid.*, p. 353.

[11] The sacrifice of human beings and livestock to accompany the dead to the other world and the burial of valuable property with the dead, not to mention the vengeance killings of men in tribes in which the belief in natural death is wanting, can scarcely be considered as anything but evil by-products of the belief in immortality.

[12] Bronislaw Malinowski, *Magic, Science, and Religion* (Boston: Beacon Press, 1948), p. 43.

[13] For a development of these views see M. F. Ashley Montagu, *On Being Human*, rev. ed. (New York: Hawthorn Books, 1966); M. F. Ashley Montagu, *The Direction of Human Development* (New York: Hawthorn Books, 1970).

[14] *Nicomachean Ethics,* I, vii. 15.

[15] *Ibid.,* X, vii. 8.

[16] Fred Hoyle, *The Nature of the Universe* (New York: Harper and Row, 1951), p. 139.

[17] Georg Brandes, *Nietzsche* (London: Heinemann, 1914), p. 19.

[18] James T. Shotwell, "Mechanism and Culture," in *Science and Man,* ed. by R. N. Anshen (New York: Harcourt, Brace & World, 1942), p. 157.

CHAPTER 4

An Anthropologist Looks at Religion

Every religion is good that teaches man to be good.
—Thomas Paine, *Rights of Man*

I SUPPOSE one of the most frequent questions the anthropologist is asked by the inquiring layman is whether primitive peoples have religion. This is akin to another question frequently asked of the anthropologist, namely, whether the languages of primitive people have a grammar. Since grammar constitutes the formal rules by which words are used to convey meanings, it should be fairly obvious that all languages must have a grammar. I should, in passing, mention here for the sake of the record that I have encountered a candidate for the Ph.D. degree in philology who was quite unaware of this fact. The layman may therefore breathe more easily. Religion is the grammar of the human soul. Just as grammar constitutes the formal rules by which meanings are conveyed in language, so religion constitutes the system of formal rules by which man relates to the universe in which he finds himself. This is a rather broad definition of religion, and under its terms modern science could be described as a religion; indeed, it has become for many people the god of the common man's idolatry.

It cannot be too often pointed out that definitions can be meaningful only at the end of an inquiry rather than at the beginning of one. In any event, religion is too complex an area of human experience to be circumscribed by a narrow definition. The inquiries of anthropologists and others during the last eighty years have yielded the quality that appears to be universally the essence of religion. This was stated by the English anthropologist Edward Burnett Tylor in 1871 in his book *Primitive Culture* in his minimum definition of religion as the belief in spiritual beings. The belief in spiritual beings was called by Tylor *animism*. I know of no society in which the belief in supernaturals has been absent. It might occur to some that Communist Russia is such a society. But, indeed, Communist Russia affords an excellent example of the seemingly inherent tendency of the human mind toward religious behavior. Communist Russia, of course, has a full-panoplied pantheon of deities and other supernaturals. Karl Marx occupies the position of the supreme god, god the father; Lenin occupies the position of god the son. Now that Stalin is dead he will, no doubt, become the holy ghost, while his living replacement becomes the temporal representative of these supernormal powers on earth. The development of Confucianism is a historically older illustration of the same religious process. Confucius (Kiung Tzu, 551–479 B.C.) was a paid public teacher and a distinguished historian whose moral philosophy was based on human relationships, without reference to supernaturals of any kind. Confucius founded no religion, but it was not long before his later followers converted his teachings into a religious system. Filial piety and the memory of parents, parents and ancestors to whom one was responsible for one's conduct and whom one revered as in other religions one revered the deity, readily paved the way for the emotional attitude that combines both the elements of relatedness to and control of and by the powers that are in the universe. Personified in the form of parents and in the principle "He who loves his parents hates no man; he who reveres his parents is discourteous to no man," the religion of Confucianism came into being without a belief in God. But soon the religious beliefs of ancient China began to invade the new religion. In the course of 350 years, that is, by the time the Emperor Wu Ti (140–87 B.C.) had elevated Confucianism to a national religion, "It had already incorporated all the traditional beliefs and superstitions of ancient China which such naturalistic philosophers as Confucius had tried to destroy or purify" (Hu Shih). Confucius had become sanctified.

With the secularization of religion it is not impossible that in the United States we may similarly achieve the sanctification of George Washington and Thomas Jefferson. Certainly the Constitution is already on its way toward achieving the status of the Unread Testament, which everyone knows about but which very few know.

While the belief in supernaturals may be said to form the core of the religious state, the religious state itself everywhere takes the form of an emotionally felt relatedness to forces and powers outside oneself, forces or powers that to a large extent control us and that to some extent we can influence. Such a description of religion defines its character both for the individual and society. It refers to the bond that binds the individual to the universe in which he finds himself and thus to everything that is in it, to things and persons as well as to supernaturals.

It may be noted that it was Francis Bacon (1561–1626) who was among the first to recognize, as he put it, that religion is the main bond of human society ("Religio praecipium humanae societatis vinculum," *Sermones Fideles*). This bond or relatedness was already breaking down in the Western world when Francis Bacon was writing, and we are the heirs of the almost terminal breakdown of religion, a breakdown that may be traced partly to the collapse of feudalism, partly to the development of the Reformation, and largely to the undermining effects of science. I am not implying that these developments were "bad." They seem to have been inevitable. The important task for us is to understand them and their effects and to do what we can about correcting some of the excesses that have been committed in the name of science and materialism.

The idea of relatedness as involved in the nature of the religious emotion is implied by the etymology of the word "religion." Cicero derived the word from the verb *religere*, to read over again or to do over again painstakingly and by means of repeated effort. Modern scholars, on the other hand, derive the word from *religare*, to bind or to bind together.

What have anthropologists to say concerning the origins of religion? This is a question about which anthropologists, like other people, can only speculate. They have, however, the advantage of being able to utilize the evidence of the possible origins of religion derived from the study of nonliterate peoples. Nonliterate people are so called because they have no written history. Such people are no longer called "primitive" by anthropologists because the only thing primitive about them is likely to be their technology; otherwise they may often be in many respects culturally very much more complex than we are. It is important to be quite clear

about the fact that so far as their mental capacities are con-
cerned·all peoples would appear to possess similar average
potentialities. The cultural differences that exist between
them are not to be accounted for on the basis of innate mental
differences. On the other hand, the anthropologist finds that
most of the cultural differences one encounters among the
different peoples of the earth are to be explained as due to
differences in the history of their experience and not to innate
factors of any kind. When then we look to nonliterate peoples
and their cultures for some light upon the possible origins of
religion, we do so not because we think that they are mentally simple but because they are culturally more illuminating
in some respects than ourselves.

There have been many theories concerning the origin of
religion. Herbert Spencer thought that it arose out of ancestor worship, Frazer out of magic, Marett out of awe, fear,
and wonder of the supernatural or *pre-animism*, and Howells
as a normal psychological adjustment by which societies
build a barrier of fantasy against fear. Durkheim regarded
religion as the most primitive of all social phenomena. "It
is out of it," he wrote, "that there have come, by successive
transformations, all the other manifestations of collective
activity, law, morality, art, science, political forms, etc. In
the beginning, all is religious." According to Durkheim the
origin of the religious experience was to be sought in the
collective euphoria engendered when individuals came together in large gatherings of the tribe, in reaction to the
rather arid, dull, and languishing experience of secular life.
Andrew Lang believed that religion originated with the belief
in high gods. No doubt there is something of truth in most
of these theories. All that the anthropologist can at present
do is to point out the limitations of each of them and be

grateful for the light they have helped to throw upon the nature of religion.

The anthropologist surveying the great variety of patterns of human experience as he finds them at the present time has great difficulty in reconstructing the history of that experience. But one thing is clear in the study of the religious experience: The universe is presented to every people as something of a mystery, a universe of transcendental but powerful forces. And in every people of which we have any knowledge we find the individual and the group striving to relate themselves to these powerful forces. Such cravings are found to be universal, and to this elementary subjective experience we usually give the name "spiritual."

It is an interesting reflection that this craving to relate oneself to the mysterious forces of the universe, to reveal and to bring into harmonic order something of its mystery, is precisely the same attitude of mind to which we give the name "scientific." It is in the means, the method, by which these attitudes are realized that the differences between science and religion are produced. The method of religion is private acquiescence in the public solution of the mystery, whereas science is characterized by public acquiescence in the private solution of the mystery. Religion is a social communion in which the individual joins; science is essentially the continuous creation of the individuals who have privately pursued their devotions but who have had to submit to having them publicly verified before they could be accepted. The method of religion is faith; the method of science is doubt. Faith is certainty without proof. Science is proof without certainty. Religion as experience is subjective; science as experience is objective—or at least attempts to be. Religion is revelatory; science is demonstrative. But when all this has been said, even at these areas of difference the resemblances between religion and science are substantial. The substantiality of the differences, however, must not be underestimated.

But to return to the anthropologist's "vision." The anthropologist, as he has come closer to the person in the field, to the individual member of society, has found that the person in society at once feels very close to and very far from his fellow man, but there is always the strongest desire to be related to one's fellow man. Human beings have devised no more successful means of achieving this relatedness to one's fellow human beings than religion. When there is combined the emotional experience of the world in which one finds oneself as mystery, with the craving to solve some part of that mystery by identification with the powers that be, with the feeling of relatedness and loneliness, one has something of the matrix out of which the religions of all people grow.

Studies at home and in the field have turned up strong evidence suggesting that the objective forms we tend to give our religions are greatly influenced by our experience as persons. This ought to sound like a truism. I hope it does. For example, the experience of children within the family, with their parents in particular, would seem to be closely related to the kind of gods different peoples create. For to many of us it seems that our gods and goddesses, our devils and witches, are to a large extent the projections of our parental figures. Anthropologists, indeed, have studied the relation of the parental disciplines imposed in particular societies to the development of the security system of the individual. Since religion, it is argued, forms part of the security system of the group, the parental disciplines are bound to be reflected in the religion. Abram Kardiner, a psychiatrist, and Ralph Linton, an anthropologist, jointly started out with the hypothesis that the technique used to solicit aid from the super-natural powers must in every way conform to the character of the disciplines imposed on the child by its disciplinarians. Kardiner and Linton tested these hypotheses on several different cultures and have convincingly shown their value. This is an interesting aspect of modern anthropological investigation, which is not too well known. Let us therefore deal with their findings.

Among the Tanala of Madagascar and the Marquesans there is some emphasis on early sphincter control in the disciplining of children. If the child learns control he is approved; if he fails he is disapproved. A basic constellation of emotions is created in the child: "If I do as is expected of me I will be approved." It is culturally demanded of the child that he be orderly and clean. This becomes a constellation of obedience; later it may become one of responsibility and conscientiousness. If the child does what is required of him and he finds himself rewarded, a working balance may be struck. If, however, he is obedient and remains unrewarded, increased anxiety and inhibition or pugnacity and defiance may result.

The situation that creates this series of constellations in the individual the anthropologist calls the "primary institution." Out of the experience of such institutions or situations will grow the conviction that obedience brings protection. The power of the parent becomes inflated as that of the child becomes deflated. When, as an adult, the individual is confronted with a situation in which he feels himself helpless and supplicates aid from the supernatural powers, he is already in possession of the technique for securing the aid of the superior being. He can secure that aid by obedience or by a system of reinstatement techniques, such as punishment, fine, and sacrifice in the sense of self-deprivation, all of which, as Kardiner and Linton say, are derived from his actual experience. In this way the "secondary institution," that is, the religious practice or ritual, becomes a product not of the primary institution directly, but of the constellation of emotions that have been conditioned in the individual by the primary institution. This constellation the individual automatically falls back upon whenever he finds himself in a situation like the original one. The religious practices in fact have no resemblance directly to the toilet training practices of his infancy, but the actual religious practices can be understood principally in terms of the early constellation of emotions produced by these early parental disciplinary acts.

Quite independently of Kardiner and Linton, Bateson and Mead found that in Bali child-rearing practices were highly correlated with religious ideas and practices. Attitudes toward children are projected upon the gods. In Bali the gods are thought of as the children of the people, and they address the people as "mama" and "papa." The people spoil and indulge their gods just as in many ways they do their children. But the children also receive a good deal of frustration, particularly during the lengthy nursing period at the mother's breast. The father, on the whole, is the more embracing and permissive parent. It is not surprising, therefore, to find the mother represented in ceremonial theatrical performances as the witch and the father as the kindly dragon who is opposed to the witch.

More recent studies in the field tend to support such correlations between parental discipline and the forms of religious belief. But we don't have to leave home in order to make this kind of analysis. The history and being of Christianity will serve our purposes very well. Christ was born into a society in which its dominant patriarchal structure gave the father tyrannical power over his family. This is well brought out in the Old Testament. The god of the Old Testament is a tyrannical father. In keeping with the subservient position of women among the Old Testament Jews, there are no female gods or minor female deities in the Jewish religion. The yearning for a loving father, which all children develop who have not had one, is to be seen expressed in the teaching and conduct of Christ. It may be suspected that the wide appeal which Christianity has had has in part been due to the fact that the central figure constitutes a father-image of love, a god of love. A god of love who, in keeping with the repressed fears of those who have been disciplined by tyrannical fathers, loves his children so much that he is even willing to sacrifice his only begotten son for them. Sons who have been sacrificed by their own fathers and who, as fathers themselves, may sacrifice their own sons, understandably find something attractive and satisfying in such a conception. For here one can at once have a father who is genuinely a father of love, a father whom one wished one's own father could have been, together with a filial relationship that is reminiscent of one's own and that may unconsciously be realized in relation to one's son.

The elevation in status women underwent as a result of the projection of the loving mother in the figure of Mary has been found not unsatisfying both by women and men.

The life of the gods would seem to be but the life of man, unconscious and conscious, writ large, the life of man as he is, as he aspires to be.

The rise of materialism and the wholesale rejection of religion during the late nineteenth century may not be unrelated to the widespread failure of the child's authority figures, principally the father and in part the mother, to provide him with much-needed love, so that when science began challenging the orthodoxies, it was easy for the adult to reject the beliefs of his father by calling upon his repressed rebellion against the father figure.

With the humanization of fathers and of mothers, we may expect a return to some form of religion, whether profane or otherwise.

Philosophers of religion have defined any experience of the person in relation to his god as religious. Such a definition is possible only to philosophers; the anthropologist knows that there are peoples who have no gods but who are at least as religious as the most religious peoples known to us. The Australian aborigines, for example, are a deeply religious people, but they have no gods. If you ask the central Australian aborigines of the Arunta tribe who created the world they will tell you that in the *alchera,* that is, in the far, far away dream time, there dwelt in the western sky two beings, of whom you will be told that they are *Numbakulla,* that is, self-existing beings who came out of nothing. *Numbakulla* are formless beings. They did not create the world—the Arunta do not presume to know who did—it all happened so long ago in the time of dreaming, in the *alchera.* It happened one day that *Numbakulla* discerned, far away to the east, a number of *Inapertwa,* that is, rudimentary human beings or incomplete ones, who possessed neither limbs nor senses, who did not eat, and who each presented the appearance of a somewhat formless human being, all doubled into a rounded mass in which just the vague outlines of the various parts of the body could be seen. These *Inapertwa,* who were destined to be transformed into men and women by the *Numbakulla,* represented the intermediate stage in the transformation of animals and plants into men, so that when the *Numbakulla* came down to earth and fashioned the *Inapertwa* into human beings, each individual so fashioned naturally retained an intimate relationship with the animal, plant, or other object of which he was indirectly a transformation and with which he was at one time identical. It is in this way that human beings came into existence, and it is for this reason that they possess totems, that is, an animal, plant, or other object or thing, such as water, wind, sun, fire, cloud, and so on, with which each individual is closely identified, since it is to that plant, animal, object, or thing that the aboriginal believes himself to owe his original creation.

These beliefs are not only religious but they also constitute an account of the creation which also comes close to satisfying all the requirements of a theory of evolution—a scientific theory of the evolution of human beings, for there is very good reason to believe that this creation account is at least in part based on very close observation of the characters of unborn young taken out of the wombs of animal mothers and also upon those of prematurely born human embryos and fetuses. However this may be, it is quite certain that the Arunta do not regard *Numbakulla* as gods, they enter into no communion with them, and to them they offer no sacrifices or worship; in fact, *Numbakulla* no longer exist.

The Australian aborigines have no gods, but they have a full-fledged religion in their cosmogony, their belief in guardian spirits, prayer, sacrifice, and the existence of the soul. The criterion of sacredness for the aboriginal is the totem, but it is not the totem as such that is sacred but what might be called its principle or spiritual essence. It is this essence that renders the totem sacred. Durkheim has claimed that totemism is the most primitive form of religion. This is doubtful, for we know of many peoples who exhibit no evidences of ever having passed through a totemic stage of development—however, we cannot be certain.

The spiritual principle or totemic principle that we encounter in aboriginal religious belief we also encounter among many other nonliterate peoples. This supernatural power was first described by Bishop Codrington among the Pacific Melanesians, who called it *mana*. *Mana* is a supernatural power or influence responsible for everything beyond the power of men and is outside the common processes of nature. "It is present in the atmosphere of life, attaches itself to persons and things, and is manifested by results which can only be ascribed to its operation. When one has got it he can use it and direct it, but its force," wrote Codrington, "may break forth at some new point; the presence of it is ascertained by proof." Thus, if a stone has roughly the shape of some animal, tucked under one's belt the wonderful power, the *mana*, of the stone will bring success in the hunt. If it has the shape of a fruit, buried in the ground it will greatly increase the normal yield. Anyone and anything can have *mana;* there is no predicting what will and what will not have *mana*. But one thing is certain: Some things and some people, for some unknown reason, just do not have it. Having *mana* is a matter of luck, but *mana* certainly is not luck itself, as one modern anthropologist has suggested. The idea of luck largely does not exist among most nonliterate peoples, the aleatory element, the element of chance as it is understood among ourselves, is practically unknown, for in nonliterate societies everything as a rule has a determinate cause. *Mana* is an attribute or quality of supernatural power inherent in a thing itself or becomes so by attaching itself to something. It works of itself; one doesn't have to manipulate it or enter into any relation of any kind with it. It is this difference that distinguishes it from animism, that is, the active entry into relations with the spirits. *Mana* is powerful *per se*, spirits only contingently so.

Precisely similar conceptions are found all over the world but are most clearly and sharply defined in the Melanesian concept of *mana*, which is not a term that designates supernatural beings but refers to an impersonal wonderful power that may be likened to the supernatural voltage with which the universe is charged. Not all people make a clear distinction between this power as personal and this power as impersonal. For example, among American Indian tribes, the terms *manitou* (Algonquian), *orenda* (Iroquois), and *wakanda* (Sioux), which are different names for the same attribute embraced by *mana*, may be either impersonal or personal and may mean either supernatural power in the abstract or a supernatural power and may be applied to a holy man or to a religious practitioner. In one form or another the concept of wonderful or supernatural power is found among all peoples. Furthermore, the manipulation of this wonderful or supernatural power and the beliefs that grow out of it constitute religion.

In order to make the world intelligible to himself, man creates it anew in terms of his own experience; he brings the world, as it were, under domestication. The figures he projects into it are images compounded of the moral necessities that the authority figures of his experience, whether in the form of parents, teachers, or conscience, have urged upon him. As Ruth Benedict has put it:

> He sees in the external world the playing out of a human drama actuated by moral significance; that is, he sees it humanly directed toward rewarding those who have performed their required obligations and denying those who have failed in them. He is no longer in a blind and mechanistic universe. This wishful thinking, which is embodied in the religions of the world, and is worked out conceptually

in mythology and theology and behavioristically in the religious techniques of petition and rapport, ranks with the great creations of the human mind.

In these religious techniques is inherent the imperative urge of the believer to act—to act according to the requirements of his beliefs and the nature and meaning of the universe as revealed to him. It is the urge to act in this way that constitutes the moral and social implication of all true religious experience and gives rise to the religious techniques universally found in human groups: *magic*, the attempt to compel the supernatural; *reverence*, the combination of awe and love and admiration that one offers to the supernatural powers; *divination*, or control by foreknowledge of supernatural power; *sacrifice*, or control by gift, in which one puts the supernaturals under the compulsion to repay the gift by doing what one wants, or else by simply pleasing the supernaturals; *taboo*, or control by abstention because of the dangerousness of the supernaturals; *fetishes* and *amulets*, covering two aspects of religious behavior. Supernatural power treated as an attribute of objects makes amulets of those objects. When the seat of spirits or objects are treated in their animistic guise they constitute fetishes; there is also the belief in *guardian spirits*, with whom you may enter into communion either at his service or at yours.

Compulsion and rapport are the two extremes of religious behavior with which one enters into relation with the supernaturals. Between these extremes there is every possible degree of compulsion and rapport or combination of both. *Prayer*, or communication with the supernaturals through speech, is the last of the religious forms of behavior or techniques that must be mentioned.

It is not possible here to examine in greater detail each

of these forms of religious behavior. They are mentioned here as being forms of behavior found in all religious systems of which we have knowledge. The forms religions assume in different human groups are as various as they could possibly be, and so is the pervasiveness of religion in any culture. For example, among the Polynesian Samoans supernaturalism is at a minimum, whereas it virtually occupies the whole life of the Polynesian Maori of New Zealand. On the whole, non-literate peoples are more profoundly religious than civilized peoples. Among the Zuni Indians of the American Southwest religion is highly formalized, whereas among the Chuckches of Siberia it is by comparison informal. This brings us to the matter of *ceremonialism*. Ceremonialism is not inevitably rooted in religious faith, but it is a form of behavior usually, though not always, associated with religious acts. It may be defined as a body of formal and sanctioned observances, learned by observation or precept, indicating an attitude of reverence toward the supernatural. Ceremonialism takes on the character of *ritual* when the order of words or the pattern of behavior is thought to have inherent virtue or power to produce results. In its secular form ceremonialism becomes pageantry. Secular pageantry has, of course, often been taken over for the purposes of religious ceremonialism. The function of both ceremonialism and ritual is essentially collective or group participation in the solemnization of collective behavior, to yield a collective sense of the importance of that behavior.

Although the religious systems of the Western world (indeed, all the higher ethical religions) are concerned with the conflict between good and evil, many of the nonliterate religions are more or less unconcerned with this aspect of life. In such cultures the relatedness the individual feels toward his supernaturals may, insofar as his fellow men are concerned, be dealt with in secular terms, and ethical sanctions may be largely a matter of secular concern, though religious sanctions may often be massed behind them at many points. Religion and morality are not, however, identified in such cultures. In our own culture we are witnessing at one and the same time the emergence of a strong secular conception of morality based on science and experience and, on the other hand, a return to revealed religion and some of its more secularized counterparts, such as in the various reformed versions of Christianity. Indeed, we live in an age in which it is already possible to perceive the lines along which the fundamental tenets of revealed religion and an ethics based on scientifically discovered principles may be fruitfully joined—a sort of scientific humanism.

To conclude: We see that universally men have evolved religious systems in which religious behavior has repeatedly and independently been calculated to secure similar ends. This fact bears testimony to the unity of the human mind Everywhere the religious experience creates the atmosphere and the attitudes that enable human beings to regulate their conduct in the world within which they find themselves. With the development and deepening of the meaning of the religious experience in history within the matrix of an increasingly complex social world, human beings begin to understand that communion with the supernaturals must be extended to communion with one's fellow human beings and finally to a universally moral obligation of fellowship.

The anthropologist, at least this anthropologist, sees the freedom to develop and subscribe to any religion one chooses in a free democracy leading to the democratization of religion and thus gradually to closer understanding between peoples, which rigid orthodoxies have hitherto prevented. In the religions of the world he sees the struggle of humanity toward the attainment of the community of man, in the reverence for life and the destiny of man which, in a mysterious universe, slowly leads man to the discovery of the principle that the way of humanity must ineluctably be through the path of love.

CHAPTER 5

Cultural Development and Religion

RELIGION IS the aspect of human conduct concerned with the fundamental relation of man to his fellows, to the great issues of life and death, salvation, immortality, and to the universe in which he lives. For the greater part of man's history and for the greater part of mankind up to the present moment, religion has provided both a moral system and an explanation of the sources of life and morality and of the goals of human life and the meaning of existence. In the service of this task most religions have called upon supernatural devices to assist them. From the earliest times it would appear that a principal industry of men has been the manufacture of supernaturals.

The emotional need of human beings to relate themselves not only to other human beings but to virtually everything to which they can possibly relate themselves, whether present to sense or not, is quite as powerful as the pressures that cause human beings to seek the satisfaction of their most basic needs. And this is the fundamental meaning of the truth that man cannot live by bread alone. Being beyond all other things the symbol-using animal and being man by virtue of being the symbol-using animal, humanity has always and will always seek to relate itself through symbolic means to whatever it is that it cannot otherwise relate to.

Clearly the world is for most human beings a mystery, and quite as clearly religion has provided, if not always a satisfactory solution, at any rate a more or less satisfying explanation of that mystery. At the same time it has supplied mankind with the sanctions for the conduct it has prescribed, and by ritual and ceremonial prayer and worship, it has assisted the individual to feel part of a fellowship, the bonds of which would sustain him not only through life but also through death and afterward.

Thus religion has played probably the most important of all the roles as the great integrating, the great binding, force in the history of humanity. To dismiss religion as an "obsessional neurosis," as Freud has done, in the light of that fact, seems to me an extraordinary misunderstanding of the nature of religion. It seems to me, on the other hand, that religion is as natural a development as any other of man's cultural activities, his social organization, his tools, his legal and educational institutions, and so on. Man's religion is as natural a response to his emotional and intellectual needs as are his responses to his need for tools, the regulation of marriage, the conduct of children in relation to their elders, the relations of different families to one another, and the like.

Just as man's tools or his social institutions in the early phases of their development are primitive and in the course of time and with the accumulation of experience undergo further development, so it is with man's religious beliefs. At the present time there exist many peoples who are still living in a Stone Age technological culture, and their religious beliefs are in a parallel state of development. At the same time there exist numerous peoples who are technologically highly developed but whose religious beliefs are probably more closely related to those of the Stone Age than they are to the Age of Science.

It has, indeed, often been remarked of late years that our scientific development has far outstripped our moral development. This can hardly be doubted. Possibly the human brain is a malignant tumor that is gradually destroying the human soul. But this *may* be doubted. In any event, there seems good reason to believe that religious development has not kept abreast of development in other fields. And when one inquires into the reason for this one soon discovers the answer. It is that religion generally has built into its very structure the factors that inhibit development. Demanding implicit belief while at the same time claiming to have the answers, religion closes the minds of its adherents instead of opening them. In this lies the fundamental difference between religion and science, for the method of science is that of free and open inquiry. In the very method of science there is implicit the knowledge that there are no such things as final answers and that knowledge is infinitely perfectible. It is not, therefore, surprising that in the last hundred years the advance of science has proceeded at an incomparably more rapid rate than has the development of religion. But this need not continue to be so. And it is here that I think that science can be of the greatest help.

Comparing, as an anthropologist, the religious systems of so-called primitive peoples with those of the so-called civilized peoples, I cannot help but think that in many cases the religious systems of nonliterate peoples are in every way superior to those of most civilized peoples. I mean in the sense that those religious systems enable the individual to realize himself more fully as a human being than do the religious systems of the civilized world. Religion is not the whole of the life of nonliterate man, but it constitutes a far greater and a far more important part of his life than is true of civilized man. Nonliterate man is truly more religious than civilized man. The religious beliefs of civilized man are not more complex or really more advanced than those of non-literate man—they are merely different and often are over-laid with the thoughts and coda and practices of accumulated generations, like so many strata superimposed upon one another. Accumulation is not development. This is not to deny for one moment that there has been some development in the religious systems of the West, but it is to suggest that the sheer weight of accumulated and often conflicting tradi-tions claiming supernatural sanctions has served to retard rather than to advance the development of religion in the Western world. Probably because nonliterate peoples have not undergone a similar historical experience their religions have often remained nearer the true purpose that religion exists to serve—and this, I have already said, is to help man realize himself more fully as a human being.

Ah, but that is the operative term, "a human being." What is a human being? How many of us know the answer to that question? I suppose all of us do. But our answers will be as numerous and as various as the leaves in Vallombrosa. We know that no two human beings are either physically or mentally identical, not even so-called or rather mis-called "identical twins." Variability is the rule, and there are no exceptions to this rule. We know that man takes different forms in the varieties he presents in adaptation to the environ-ments in which he has undergone long-term development, and we know that his behavioral responses to the environment are capable of being organized in an immense variety of different forms—his cultures. And up to very recently we have tended to attribute all these differences to differences inherent in the nature of different groups of mankind. It is really only in this century that we have come to suspect that while the physical differences are mostly due to inherent differences, the psychical differences are almost certainly mostly not, that even the physical differences are superficial, minor, and quantitatively very small, while the behavioral differences are largely a matter of difference in cultural experience, and finally, that the likenesses between all members of the species *Homo sapiens* are far greater than the differences. These likenesses are fundamental to the species as a whole, for they constitute the precipitate of a long evolutionary history. And I would suggest that it is not possible to understand the nature of man very profoundly unless one understands the nature of the peculiar evolutionary process mankind has undergone, of which human beings are the culmination. If religion is a path, a road, rather than an end, then it were well for those who would wish to know where that path should really lead to acquaint themselves with the route man has taken to reach his present estate. It is these evolutionary matters that I propose to consider in what follows. And, of course, I shall discuss their significance for what I think is most likely to be the future developmental direction of religion.

The principal evolutionary changes that led to the ultimate appearance of man took place during the Pliocene epoch, which began some 13 million years ago and came to an end about two million years ago. During the Pliocene vast areas of the land in which the precursors of man are believed to have evolved were deforested and turned into open savannahs. The manlike apes who were man's precursors were thus called upon, during this long secular period of time (that is, the Pliocene, which lasted for about 11 million years), to adapt themselves to the new way of life the demands of the savannah called for as compared to the different kinds of challenges presented in the forest. With few exceptions all the members of the Primates—the order of mammals to which man in company with the lemurs, tarsiers, monkeys, and apes belongs—are forest dwellers, herbivorous and frugivorous, and quadrupedal.

In the forest environment, in which the Primates as a whole have probably spent some 60 million years (or perhaps it would be more accurate to say that the Primates began their life in the forest some 60 million years ago), the Primates had become perfectly adapted. Those Primates who found themselves forced to live on the savannahs, in the new environment, had to adjust in a variety of ways very different from the modes of adaptation of their forest-dwelling relatives. Since vegetation is sparse on the treeless plains of the savannah, the first change one would be called upon to make would be in the manner of obtaining food. Instead of living off vegetation, fruits, and nuts, one would now be called upon to live off other animals, small game, birds and their eggs, little animals that one could catch with the exercise of a little ingenuity and cooperation. To make a long and what I consider a fascinating story short, those Primates that were able to negotiate their way in the new environment most effectively left behind them a larger progeny than that of less-adaptive Primates, a progeny that would increasingly be capable of making further necessary adjustments to the environment. The others did not necessarily die out; they simply went off in other directions to occupy different niches in the environment.

What changes occurred in the precursors of man? First of all was the gradual development of upright posture, for if one could free the forelimbs for using stones and implements during the chase while running after small game, one would be at so much greater an advantage than those who remained quadrupedal. A second change would be the development of the capacity to quickly make successful responses to the challenges of the environment. This is intelligence. Those animals would have been most favored who increasingly exhibited this capacity and concomitantly lost the instinctive responses that predetermine much of the behavior of the non-human animal. With the increasing development of the capacity for intelligent behavior and the loss of instincts the dependency period of the young has to be greatly increased, for this is the period in which the young of such a species will have to learn how to be a functioning being in the new dimension of a society that is principally a symbol-using society. In adaptation to the new way of life the precursors of man would be called upon to exhibit increasingly more complex forms of cooperative behavior. Hunting game, setting snares, and digging pits are activities calling for cooperative behavior of a highly organized kind, as does the subsequent distribution of the food derived from the hunt. Furthermore, with the increase in the length of the dependency period of the young there would be a high premium placed upon the possession of those qualities in the female that would enable her to minister most efficiently to her dependent child, for such females would be likely to confer higher survival benefits upon their children than females not so well endowed with the necessary sustaining qualities. Natural selection would favor both males and females who possessed the qualities of cooperation as against those who did not, and just as man is a fetalized animal in so many of his physical traits, he is also, as it were, fetalized in his psychical traits, in the sense that he exhibits a tremendous capacity for mental growth and development for a much longer period of time than any other creature.

The point I would like to emphasize is that as I see it the evolution of man is characterized by increasing plasticity or educability, with which are concomitantly associated increasing dependency and interdependency and cooperation. This triad, plasticity, dependency, and cooperation, comprises the three great qualities that led to the evolution of man and in man's own evolution as man have played a dominant role. It should surely be obvious that if man is the most dependent and the most plastic or educable of creatures he must also be, if he is to survive, the most cooperative, for unless he receives a maximum amount of cooperation he could not survive for any durable period of time during his first half-dozen years, nor could he learn to be a functioning human being. While all three elements (plasticity, dependency, and cooperation) are present to some extent in all animals, they have reached their highest development in man. Most of us understand that man is the most educable and the most dependent of creatures, but what we do not seem to understand is that he is also the most cooperative, that if we separate the necessity for cooperation from the plasticity and dependency requirements of man we do the greatest violence possible to his development as a human being. Indeed, without cooperation neither the dependency nor plasticity needs of the individual can be satisfied, and if under such a deficiency exposure he manages somehow to survive, it is as a crippled human being rather than as a healthy human being, as a creature who has been deprived of his birthright, which is development as a healthy human being. The whole of human experience bears testimony to the importance of cooperation for the development of man, but it is only within the last few decades that science has been bringing the support of its discoveries to that testimony.

In studying the mother-child relationship in relation to the subsequent development of the mother and her child we discover that the cooperative organization of humanity is best seen in its most highly developed form in the relationship of the mother to her child, the relationship that we call love. It is in the mother-child relationship that is to be perceived the hearth and the home of the Golden Rule, to do unto others as you would have them do unto you. The relationship between mother and child is symbiotic. It is not interrupted at birth, as some of our medicine men have tried to persuade us, but becomes increasingly more complex at birth, for at this juncture the symbiotic relationship ceases to be principally biological and physical and now becomes largely psychical. From the womb the child passes into the family, which is but an extension of the womb, and from the family the individual must be prepared to pass into the community, and from the community into the nation, and from the nation into the community of nations, and from the community of nations into the universe of which he is of the very selfsame stuff.

These transitions from the womb to the family and its extensions can only be made through the love with which every mother is normally equipped, as a long result of the evolutionary process, to give her child. This fact is recognized in the sayings of many peoples and perhaps most succinctly in the ancient Eastern saying that since God could not be everywhere he created mothers. The mother of the human species is endowed with the kind of capacities for love that so conspicuously characterize her because the young of human kind needs that love more than anything else in the world in order to grow and develop in his capacities for being human.

This is not rhetoric but demonstrable and verifiable psycho-physical fact.[1] The member of the species *Homo sapiens* who is not adequately loved during his first half dozen years is severely handicapped in his development as a human being for the rest of his life, for he has failed to receive those stimulations to development that are so necessary if he is to become what he is capable of becoming, namely, one who confers survival benefits upon others in a creatively enlarging manner, one for whom to live and love is one.

This, it seems to me, is what the whole course of human evolution has led to, namely, that human beings shall relate to each other as a loving mother relates to her dependent child. Such relatedness has had the highest selective value for the human species in all societies and in all times, and if men fail to recognize this, or once having learned this truth ever forget it, they will from that moment on be in imminent danger of destroying themselves. Just as the mother's love is physiologically and psychologically necessary for the sur-vival and development of the child, so love is necessary to the survival and development of human beings all the days of their lives, for (to quote George Chapman, 1559–1634):

Love is Nature's second sun,
Causing a spring of virtues where he shines.

Every human being is born with a built-in system of values, the basic needs, all of which are oriented in the direction of love. The infant is born wanting to love and to be loved. He is born with the ability to confer survival benefits in a creatively enlarging manner upon his mother and reciprocally to receive similar benefits from her. His first act in this life is to give, to give to his mother those benefits of which she stands so much in need immediately after the birth of her child, and it is only second to his giving that he receives from her from whom all blessings flow the first savor of the milk of human kindness. And it is through the stimulus of this interchange that the young of human kind is stimulated to grow and develop in his own capacities for love.

It is in this mother-child relationship that I see the workshop of future religion and the *fons et origo* of all morality, for in that relationship is inherent as a clear precipitate the whole of human psychical evolution and the crystal-clear indications of the direction in which human beings must proceed if they are to realize their evolutionary destiny, which is to live as if to live and love were one.

It is a perverse view of human nature, which too many of our Western religious systems have foisted upon an only too guilt-laden, anxious, and pietistic branch of humanity, that human nature is originally sinful and nasty "in the flesh," that innate depravity is indissolubly part of man's heritage, and that in Adam's fall we sinned all. This is, of course, an easy explanation of man's naughtiness, and it is a very common way of explaining almost anything about man to fall back upon the device of its being innate. To attribute the obscurely understood to the even more obscurely understood is one of the most ancient of man's artful dodges. The truth is that when we inquire as scientists into the nature of human nature we find no evidence whatever of any innate nastiness or hostility or aggressiveness or sinfulness or any other of the whole calendar of evils that have been attributed to the defenseless human babe.

Nor is it true, as some putatively more enlightened thinkers have come to hold, that man is born neither good nor evil, but that he is born a kind of *tabula rasa* upon which we can inscribe whatsoever we will by way of good and evil. On the other hand, as I see the evidence man is born with all his drives oriented in the direction of goodness and growth and development in goodness. The evidence for this statement is now, I believe, bombproof and it is available to anyone who cares to take the trouble to verify it for himself.

By goodness I mean the process of conferring survival benefits upon others in a creatively enlarging manner. And I use the words "goodness," "love," and "cooperation" as essentially meaning this. In short, what I am saying is that man has evolved as a creature in whom goodness has been his most valuable adaptive quality, that he is born with this quality as the central sun of his being, around which all the other needs revolve like the planets of the solar system around the sun, that he is born to love and be loved, and that all else that he is born with and develops is secondary to this. That to be a warm, loving, human being who relates himself in a creatively enlarging manner to himself and to others is beyond everything else the first and most important realization of the self. The self grows and develops in its relatedness to others, and by being loved by others develops in its capacity to love. This growth in goodness I see as the only real personal salvation and the basis and focus of what I should consider the only genuine religion, namely, the religion of goodness. Those who are interested and are capable of doing so will have to decide, upon the evidence, for themselves whether their goodness is to be their religion or whether their religion is to be their goodness. Whether God is love, or whether love is God. Whether we will continue to suspend our gods in the heavens or whether we shall be willing to bring them down to earth. Whether we shall continue to be part of the problem or whether we shall endeavor to make ourselves part of the solution.

I foresee the development of religion in the future as a consistent part of the cultural development of the person based on a more accurate and more thorough understanding of the nature of human nature than humanity has enjoyed in the past. A man's religion will be the development of his goodness and not the subscription to a traditionally organized system of superstitions, which, like so many bunions, have impeded the pilgrims' progress.

When we have understood the meaning of the value system that is built into the very nature of man and with which he is born, the value system constituted by his basic needs, and when we have understood that all these needs are, in terms of development, oriented in the direction of love, we shall perhaps for the first time understand that in this view of the nature of man's needs we have a unifying principle, which, like the principle of gravitation, brings together so much that is at present separated. Education, ethics, law, and religion all become different aspects of one and the same thing, namely, the ordering of man's growth and development in goodness.

From my point of view it will be evident that I do not think that we have much in the Western world today that resembles education. We have a great deal of instruction. But instruction is not education. Instruction is training in the use of the three "r's." Education is a causing to grow, a nourishing in the capacity to be a warm, loving human being, and the three "r's" are merely techniques in the service of that end, the end of goodness. I conceive of ethics and of law in precisely the same manner. The only relations between men that are good are loving, and the only law that is just is love, and the only worship that is true is love. This is the law and the commandment of man's nature.

NOTES

¹ The evidence will be found in some detail in M. F. Ashley Montagu, *The Direction of Human Development*, rev. ed. (New York: Hawthorn Books, 1970). See also John Bowlby, *Maternal Care and Mental Health* (Geneva: World Health Organization, 1951); John Bowlby, *Attachment and Separation* (New York: Basic Books, 1969).

CHAPTER 6

World Problems, World Religions, One World

THERE IS a story told of two Western Christian missionaries who were walking together in some part of the Orient. Suddenly they came in sight of a Buddhist temple under construction. "Ah!" said one of them in a disgusted voice, "I hate to see that! Another fortress of the enemy." "Well," said the second missionary, "I'm not so sure. I would rather be inclined to say: Another witness to man's search for God —and thank God for it!"

This is in the spirit of the poor Tibetan wanderer whom Marco Pallis encountered (as narrated in his memorable book *Peaks and Lamas*) and who after an exchange of greetings inquired of the European traveler, "And to what sublime religion do you belong?" To that poor Tibetan wanderer all religions were equally sublime, each representing but a different route to the attainment of the same eternal truths. This is the truth enshrined in the story of the two missionaries, and it is the truth all human beings must learn in one world represented by so many routes that men have hewn out of their experience in their search for wholeness.

Men have now reached the point in their history—at least some branches of mankind have—where they are beginning clearly to see that all the different routes lead to the same place—the place at which men meet on the common ground of their humanity and understand that each is involved, inseparably involved, in the other.

More than nine-tenths of the history of mankind has been the story of small, comparatively minute, populations widely separated from one another, wandering over the face of the earth, and departing further and further from each other, until for millennia they became and remained isolated from one another. It is partly in this way that the major and ethnic groups (the so-called races) of mankind came into being. During the last few thousand years the reverse process has been occurring, and men, instead of becoming separated from one another, are at an increasingly accelerating pace coming together more and more closely. One can send a message around the world in seven seconds, and no place is so distant from another that it cannot be reached within two days by jet-propelled plane. The world has indeed physically become one, and the world's problem is that a great part of humanity has not yet understood that it too must become socially one if it is to realize its evolutionary destiny.

The great tragedy of the world at the present time is that while the greatest part of mankind has desired, and, indeed, has long been anxious to clasp the hand of our fellow men everywhere, there remains a powerful minority of mankind that seeks to achieve its ends by grasping them by the throat instead.

I believe that the greatest enemy of humanity at the present time is the Communist Government of the Soviet Union. I say "Communist government of the Soviet Union" and not "Soviet people," for I am convinced that if the latter could be effectively reached we would find them as anxious as other people are to join hands in amity and in brotherhood with the rest of their fellow men throughout the world. This, in fact, is precisely what the Soviet Communist government holds forth as the promise of its intentions, but we who are in a position to take an objective look at its deeds have, I suspect, a more accurate conception of what its intentions really are. If we are to judge governments as we must, then the Communist government of the Soviet Union stands by its deeds condemned before the bar of justice and humanity. The tragedy of the Soviet people is that they have been so long deceived, so long enslaved to the falsenesses they have been fed by their power-intoxicated leaders and so cut off from all communication with the non-Communist world that they no longer have any means of discovering how thought-enslaved they have become. From such a vicious circular iron curtain there remains no escape—unless the curtain is somehow lifted.

At a period in the history of humanity when it is readier than it has ever been for the actualization of the vision of one world, the Communists constitute at once humanity's greatest obstacle and humanity's greatest challenge. For how we shall deal with the problem of Communism constitutes one of the greatest challenges to the free world, and it is a challenge we must take up if any of us are to survive.

The present conflict of ideologies has a long history in the misunderstanding and mismanagement of human relations. For example, since the October, 1917, Russian revolution the great powers have behaved in such a manner as to cause the Russians completely to distrust them. Instead of facing the fact and meaning of the Russian revolution and assisting the people to free themselves from the oppression of the tsars, the Allied powers attempted to abort the revolution and to do everything in their power to restore the monarchy. It is not commonly known that the Allied powers engaged in armed conflict with the Russians well into 1921. Since that time we have done very little to inspire the Russians with any confidence in us. I am not suggesting that one could have talked to the Communists at any time, but I am suggesting that the Germans who helped the Communists overthrow the government that wished to continue the war against them, and the Allied powers who were faced with this situation, acted about as intelligently as the United States did in supporting Chiang Kai-shek instead of the people of China and thus handing the Chinese people over to the Communists. Today instead of having 600,000,000 friends in China we have 600,000,000 enemies. And thus we go blundering on. If history doesn't repeat itself, obviously our political leaders do.

It is surely evident that the traditional approaches to the solution of these world problems are not only unsatisfactory but lead to disaster—"surely evident" were it not for the fact that our world leaders give little evidence of such understanding, for they go on repeating the same errors. They seem to know what is right but somehow contrive to do what is wrong. We all assert that we abhor war but somehow find ourselves dragged into and supporting it. We want peace and prepare for war. This is a very strange way of securing peace. If we want peace why don't we behave as if we do? That is, why don't we behave peacefully? Why, when we get into an argument do we fall back upon armaments and the argument of force? Is it perhaps because we really don't believe in the force of argument, but do believe in the argument of force? These are vital *not* rhetorical questions, and they demand an effective answer.

We have had many discussions of the answers that the various religions of the world have to offer to the world's

problems. Although these religious answers go far to providing the answers, they fall short of success; while they provide
the "know-why," or at least provide it in part, they fail to
provide the "know-how." It is one thing to have the knowledge, but quite another to know what to do with it.

As a student of man I am convinced that the life of man
must always be a religious life and, what is more, that the
education of man must be religious. I say this not as a man of
religion but as a scientist, a student of human nature, of man
in society. In what follows I shall speak of a religion that is
even now being revealed to us by the scientists of human
nature, a religion that may infuse new life into all existing
religions and demonstrate the fundamental unity of all.

It was Sir Thomas Browne who said that man lives by
a pure flame within him, a flame that should illumine man's
way and give warmth to his being. Here I shall endeavor to
set out, as it were, a scientist's analysis of this flame and to
show how it is the evolutionary destiny of man to nurse that
flame and increase its power. In the garish light of our modern
world those who have made the original discoveries and re-
discoveries of which I shall speak may be likened to so many
candles, which have cast the light of their own flame all
about them at the cost of their own consumption. And as is
often the case under such conditions, their light has mostly
gone unseen or has been only dimly recognized. But the
combined effect of their candle power sheds a greater and a
more beautiful light upon the nature of man than the most
powerful beacon that has yet glowed from the Broadways
and Los Alamoses of human folly.

This light is beautiful, but it is also strangely necessary
because by it we must find our way as human beings and by
it we must be warmed if we are to avoid another ice age of
the human spirit and this time almost certainly freeze to

death. *Anthropos*, man, the creature that looks upward, has looked heavenward to the sun for the light of the world, when all the time the spiritual light he seeks has been within him. What man has done has been to project the light that is within him upon the firmament where for too long his own light has been lost among the undependable stars or the lonely oases of an extended mirage. The necessities of beauty, of love, have become strange to us. We must recover them.

The beauty and the love of which I shall speak are represented by the essential nature of man, the spirit of man as revealed by the scientist.

We live in an age in which every human being living within the Western world is the inheritor of a trifold tradition concerning the nature of man that largely determines his outlook upon the world. This tradition is religious, secular, and scientific. Through the teachings of the Hebraeo-Christian tradition Western man has inherited a view of human nature that emphasizes its inherent evil, its essential badness. The original fall of man is continually being relived in Adam's descendants, and the task of religion—so it is conceived—is to make men aware of the evils to which their own nature tempts them and to lead them away from those temptations to evil. The secular tradition of the last few millennia tends to confirm the Hebraeo-Christian view of man's nature, and certainly the history of men during the last few thousand years has served to corroborate that view. Murder, rapine, war, slaughter, destruction, and treachery have characterized that history down to the present day. Such acts of goodness as men have exhibited during this period are explained as principally due to the religious and social controls that have been educated into them. Science, in the form of nineteenth-century Darwinian biology and evolutionary theory, shows that nature was, by human standards, essentially evil, that it was characterized by a competitive struggle for existence in which no quarter was given, the weakest going to the wall and the strongest surviving to leave their progeny behind them to continue the unending struggle. The fittest survived, and the unfit either died out or were reduced to insignificant numbers. "Fitness" was thought of as "the most successfully combative," so that the phrase "survival of the fittest" would more appropriately have been replaced by the phrase "survival of the fightingest." Man, as Darwin and his followers showed, was almost certainly the product of the same evolutionary factors, of "natural selection," and he as well as others went on to reason that just as man preserved within his physical structure the marks of his nonhuman ancestry, so he preserved within his psychic structure lowly drives and tendencies similarly derived from the beasts. Thus was a scientific demonstration provided of the origin of man's evil nature, his aggressiveness, hostility, and general cussedness.

Herbert Spencer, the sociologist, maintained that the findings of the Darwinists could be applied lock, stock, and barrel to man in society, that the lives of human beings in society were in practically every way a mirror of the lives competitively lived by animals in a state of nature. This doctrine, known as Social Darwinism, has had and continues to have an enormous influence upon the thought and conduct of man. It provided a scientific validation for the activities of exploiting industrialists, of colonizers concerned with assisting so-called superannuated races to depart as rapidly as possible from their homelands, which they were unable to "exploit." It gave army men a good reason for a war, since war, it was alleged, gave a natural decision as to who was worthy of survival, and it provided the individual with a morality from the consequences of which we have been suffering increasingly dangerously during the last hundred years.

With the advent of the new psychology, without a doubt the most important development in the history of our understanding of human nature, a deeper insight has been attained about the workings of human nature. Psychoanalysis or Freudianism is in large part responsible for the stimulus that has led so many modern scientists to a better understanding of human nature, and without it I would certainly not be able to present quite the kind of conclusions to be discussed here. This does not mean that I subscribe to everything that Freud has said. I do not. In fact, I cite Freud here because, in the Darwinian tradition, he arrived at the conclusion that man was an inherently hostile creature, that, indeed, he was born with an overpoweringly strong instinct of destruction, which led him increasingly to destructive acts involving both himself and others. Society, culture, and religion had all come into being and developed and were maintained in order to exercise the necessary controls over this creature that nature had endowed with such destructive energies. In general Freud considered that society, culture, and especially religion were failing. As he grew older he grew more pessimistic and finally concluded that he thought there were three impossible professions, namely, psychoanalysis, international relations, and bringing up children!

Building upon the method and discoveries of Darwin and Freud, we have developed a more accurate and more detailed understanding of the evolutionary process and of the nature of human nature.

In the first place, three generations of workers since Darwin have found that the picture of nature presented to us by the Darwinists was much overdrawn and distorted, that, far from nature being characterized by more or less continuous strife and competition, cooperation is in fact a dominant factor in the evolutionary process and in the preservation of species.[1] The picture of nature painted by the Darwinists was in far too somber colors and undoubtedly reflected something of the black competitive pall that hung over nineteenth-century industrial England like the backdrop of a Manchester factory district. Indeed, the picture of nature that the Darwinists saw was largely a projection upon nature of conditions existing among men in the highly industrialized and ruthlessly competitive societies of the West. We are only now beginning to put nature back into proper focus and to see it as a whole, together with its competitive and its cooperative processes, and to understand the nature and significance of each. And when we see nature in proper focus we see it not as "red in tooth and claw" but largely as a great and continuing interrelatedness, a harmonic, cooperative whole. It is a very different picture from that which the Darwinists bequeathed to us.

In the second place, our conception of human nature has undergone a fundamental change in the light of the ever growing body of evidence. I am accustomed to summing this up very briefly by saying that that evidence reveals that it is no longer true to say that man is born neither good nor evil, or that he is born evil, but that it is in a very positive and scientifically demonstrable sense more accurate to say that man is born good. By good I mean a creature who is equipped with drives that cause it to want to be loved and, what is equally as important, that wants to love. Furthermore, man is a creature that is not born with one iota of hostility, aggressiveness, evil, or badness within it, but is rendered susceptible to all these by the kind of socialization process it is made to undergo.

We know that a baby wants to be loved because if it isn't loved it exhibits the symptoms of such a lack-love experience. These symptoms range all the way from listlessness to death. On the other hand, when the infant is adequately loved, it develops in health and harmony. Indeed, the only way in which one ever develops as a healthy human being is to receive the proper stimulations of one's potentialities for being a loving, warm human being. These potentialities do not develop by themselves; they must be stimulated, and in the absence of the necessary stimulation they fail to develop. What is worse, failure to stimulate these potentialities results in the appearance of many pathological conditions, among which aggressiveness is prominent. And what is aggressiveness? It is nothing more or less than love frustrated. Aggressiveness appears when the organism has been deprived of the expected satisfaction of love, and aggressiveness is simply the name we give to that form of behavior that is the human being's way who has been deprived of love, of compelling that love somehow from the outside world that has refused it. Aggressiveness is a technique or mode of compelling the attention, the recognition, the love that has been denied a human being.

Such a conception of the nature of aggressiveness puts a very different complexion upon it from that with which we have customarily endowed it. Clearly, if aggressiveness is a form of love, of love frustrated and seeking to replenish itself, we do not do well or wisely to meet aggression with further aggression; rather, we should meet aggression with what it requires, namely, with love, sympathy, and understanding. If we are ever to solve the problem aggressiveness constitutes, at the personal, family, community, national, international, and world levels, then we shall succeed in doing so only when we have applied the method of love. To meet aggression with further aggression is to produce continuing aggression. To meet aggression with love is to meet the greatest of all human needs—the need for love.

Most religions of the world long ago arrived at this particular conclusion, and in the Christian tradition it is most familiar to us in the form of the Sermon on the Mount. We will recall the fifth chapter of the Gospel According to St. Matthew, verses 38 through 48:

Ye have heard that it hath been said, An eye for an eye, and a tooth for a tooth.

But I say unto you, That ye resist not evil: but whosoever shall smite thee on thy right cheek, turn to him the other also.

And if any man will sue thee at the law, and take away thy coat, let him have *thy* cloak also.

And whosoever shall compel thee to go a mile, go with him twain.

Give to him that asketh thee, and from him that would borrow of thee, turn not thou away.

Ye have heard that it hath been said, Thou shalt love thy neighbour, and hate thine enemy.

But I say unto you, Love your enemies, bless them that curse you, do good to them that hate you, and pray for them which despitefully use you, and persecute you;

That ye may be the children of your Father which is in heaven: for he maketh his sun to rise on the evil and on the good, and sendeth rain on the just and on the unjust.

For if ye love them which love you, what reward have ye? do not even the publicans the same?

And if ye salute your brethren only, what do ye more *than others?* do not even the publicans so?

Be ye therefore perfect, even as your Father which is in heaven is perfect.

And there is much else to the same effect in both the Old and the New Testaments. With respect to love, in Leviticus (19:18) in the Old Testament occurs the injunction "to love thy neighbor as thyself," and it was Christ who said that on the love of God and the love of one's neighbor "On these two commandments hang all the law and the prophets" (Matthew 22:35–40).

"To love thy neighbor as thyself" is an injunction, a commandment, that is implicit in most religious teachings, and today science validates that commandment in the most impressive of all ways, for as scientists we can now show that this is by far the best, the wisest, the healthiest, and the most efficient of all ways in which to live in relation to one's neighbor. We can show that it has been and is the evolutionary destiny of man to attain to greater and greater understanding of the role love plays in the lives of all animals, but most especially in man himself, and to apply that understanding for the benefit not alone of himself but for that also of all earth's living things. For we know now that it is inherent in the nature of protoplasm to be cooperative. The word "cooperative" is here used at perhaps a higher level of abstraction than would actually apply to the molecules constituting protoplasm, but the word does convey better than any other what I mean, and so I use it. The origin of cooperation, of love, is to be seen in the origin of one living thing from another. All living cells come into being from other living cells, and in the process of coming into being they are so related to the maternal cell as to be virtually completely dependent upon and interdependent with it. Dependency and interdependency are, in fact, the conditions that define the biological, the organismal relationship. In no other living creature does this relationship play so critical a role as in man. For man is born the most dependent of all creatures, the creature that has been entirely freed of those biological predeterminants of behavior, the instincts, which enable animals of many other species to shift for themselves at a comparatively early age. Man, uniquely, is dependent for several years upon other human beings for his survival, and he is equally entirely dependent upon other human beings for many more years in order to learn the accomplishments that enable him to lead an active life among his fellow men.

It is because of this fact, because of man's precarious dependence upon and interdependence with his fellow human beings for his development as a social human being, that it becomes so important to understand the nature of this creature called *Homo sapiens,* in order that the innate necessities of his being be properly supplied. For if those necessities are not properly supplied then the organism suffers certain psychic consequences. In short, if the organism is not properly loved then it fails to learn how to love others, becomes disoperative and aggressive, awkward and difficult to itself and to others, and very soon so absorbed in itself that it increasingly fails to be alive to the necessities of others. Such persons create great havoc in the world, in the image of the havoc that has been created in themselves.

It is of the first importance to understand, then, that the making of the world in which we live is in large part the making of human beings who have been inadequately made —inadequately made because the nature of man has been inadequately, even wrongly, understood. If, then, we are to remake the world, we must begin by remaking it not at the periphery so much as at the core—and that central core is man himself. We must realize that men are deformed and deteriorated children and that if we are to enter the kingdom of heaven—and I mean that kingdom of heaven that men can create here upon earth for themselves—we must turn to the consideration of the nature of those unintimidated, unspoiled, unrepressed, and undistorted creatures we call babies. We must learn to respect our children and not treat them as if they belonged to an inferior race, "the childish" who must learn to be "grown up" and act like their elders.

I think it may be agreed that the more we can get children to act less like their elders the better it will be for humanity and for the world. We can learn more about how adults should behave from children than we can from adults how children should behave. The newborn baby tells us clearly and unambiguously what it is that human beings need all the days of their lives: to love and be loved. And this is the law of human nature and of human relations, which, when all that has ever been written and researched and said on this subject has been completed, will remain as the essential precipitate. It is upon this essential principle of experience and reality that all the religions of the world can meet and all men communicate with one another. And it is by the application of this essential principle that virtually all human problems can be solved. Indeed, it is only by the application of this principle that world problems will be solved, that world religions will be unified without being made uniform, and that one world will become a reality.

NOTES

[1] For a brief discussion of the evidence see M. F. Ashley Montagu, *Darwin, Competition, and Cooperation* (New York: Schuman, 1952). See also W. C. Allee, *Cooperation Among Animals* (New York: Schuman, 1951).

CHAPTER 7

Morals and Moralisms

A SIMPLE and objective account of the moral ideas and practices of nonliterate peoples provides some conception of the relative differences and likenesses various people exhibit in these respects. Before proceeding with such an account a few words are in order respecting the nature and function of moral ideas in all societies. In this connection it is possible to lay down certain broad generalizations to which all societies are found to conform.

In the first place, it is evident that moral ideas have a regulative effect; they function as abstract or ideal but nevertheless very real controls of the behavior of human beings in relation to each other and to the world of institutions, objects, things, and creatures in which they find themselves.

THE BASIS OF MORAL IDEAS

In the second place, at the basis of all moral ideas is the people's conception of the "good." In whatever variety of ways it may be codified, the conception of the "good" all peoples have arrived at may be phrased in the following way: The "good" is that, and that is "good," which confers survival benefits upon the group. Such a view of the "good," and it is one that every people holds, makes it possible to bring in the analytic methods of science, philosophy, theology, psychology, and anthropology, as well as other disciplines, as a means of measuring the real value of the varieties of forms this conception assumes.

In most nonliterate societies moral ideas are functions of the magico-religious system; it is not surprising, therefore, to find an absence of abstract moral formulations as such. The moral ideas are part and parcel of the magico-religious system in which one is encultured or conditioned, and one's relation to the supernatural is an immediately personal one rather than a mediately impersonal one. Transgressions are punished by the supernaturals more because the latter have been offended than because the moral order has been transgressed. A man knows that he may be punished, that he may die, even in the absence of any knowledge of his transgression on the part of anyone else but himself. The supernaturals know, and *they* cannot be escaped. This idea, of course, is not restricted to nonliterate cultures, but is to be found in all cultures in which religious beliefs are predominant. Even where secular beliefs predominate and moral laws are codified, the effects of the codified and the uncodified laws tend in the same direction. However, it is an open question as to which is more effective in securing the regulation of conduct: *morals*, pertaining to behavior relating to the distinction between right and wrong, or *moralism*, that is, morals distinguished from religion or divested of religious teaching.

In nonliterate societies, morality functions in a predominantly magico-religious matrix; one's obligations to one's society are under strict surveillance of the supernaturals, and if one performs one's duty toward them they will do well enough by us. The relationship is a reciprocal one, and in some societies is dependent not only upon the fulfillment of human obligations but also upon the fulfillment of the obligations of the supernaturals toward man. Thus, in certain tribes of Africa and also in the Society Islands in the South Pacific, should the supernaturals fail to behave in the manner expected of them, they may be cast off and exchanged for other supernaturals.

Religion is the belief in supernaturals, magic is the belief in the ability to manipulate the supernaturals. In many nonliterate magico-religious systems there is retained something of the belief in the capacity of men to induce their gods to do their bidding. Even in a religion such as Christianity something of this belief is retained. God listens to our prayers and supplications, and one of the best ways of getting him to do what we wish is to be a good Christian according to the particular prescriptions of the sect to which we belong. But this is not the same as compelling the supernaturals to do our bidding, and this is what magic is calculated to achieve. In certain Christian sects there is a very near approximation to this, in which by auricular confession of one's sins, indulgences may be secured upon the fulfillment of certain penances. Trading with the supernaturals is no more limited to nonliterate peoples—if as much—than it is to the peoples of the Western world who have become so expert at trading with their consciences.

In brief, it is an error to assume that morality and moralism can be or are completely separated in nonliterate cultures. In every nonliterate community it is possible to find individuals who are to some extent capable of taking an objective view of some, at any rate, of the elements of their society and others who, on purely secular grounds, may find their supernaturals unsatisfactory or otherwise open to criticism. Secular moralism is influenced by magico-religious morality, whether as direct influence or as reaction. If the supernaturals don't send the desired rain, one may say, "Look here, my dear supernatural, I'm fulfilling my part of the bargain with you. I'm offering you the required sacrifices. What about you? If you don't send the rain pretty soon, I'll simply transfer my allegiance to some other supernatural who will." This is not the kind of relationship that is maintained between men and their supernaturals in all nonliterate societies, but it is in some. Reference is made here to this kind of relationship between men and their supernaturals because it brings out, in high relief as it were, something of the essential nature of the reciprocal relationship involved in all magico-religious and religious systems of belief.

It is a mistaken view, widely prevalent, that nonliterate peoples live in a constant state of terror, in abject fear of the supernaturals who are ever ready to pounce upon and punish them for their transgressions. The truth is that the magico-religious systems of nonliterate peoples, on the whole, permit people to live their lives quite as happily and as free from fear as do the most advanced religious systems of the literate peoples of the world. The morality of nonliterate peoples is a functional and fundamentally integrative, as well as regulative, factor of society and gives support to social codes or moralisms. If it is considered good to indulge in certain economic activities at certain seasons, morality will reinforce and encourage these economic practices at such seasons with the appropriate rites. Ancestor worship and respect for one's ancestors supports parental authority—which may or may not have a religious or moral sanction—while the morality of magic is such that it tends to produce greater social cohesiveness, in that a man is likely to feel more secure both in person and in property when he has available to him the instrument of magical retaliation. This belief in magic gives much support to the political authority of chiefs and headmen, for they are frequently believed to be possessed of stronger magic than that which is given to ordinary mortals.

DEATH

The great issues of life and death are in all societies dealt with in a fundamentally similar manner. In some nonliterate societies the death of a human being is regarded as unnatural, in the sense that it is thought to have been produced by another person. This belief exists among most Australian aboriginal tribes. Death, it is believed, is produced by black magic, that is, by sorcery, and the idea is to track down the murderer and see to it that he is adequately punished. The murderer is generally held to be a member of another tribe, and by the proper methods of divination it is generally possible to discover him. Such beliefs and practices occur among many other nonliterate peoples. It should also be pointed out that there are many areas of Europe at the present time in which similar beliefs and practices may be found among some segments of the population.

Murder is universally regarded as a crime, and is usually punishable by death, although in all societies a successful plea of self-defense frees the accused of any imputation of murder. However, in many nonliterate societies even though the accused killed in self-defense, he is required to make restitution in the form of a settlement of some sort with the family of the bereaved. In still other nonliterate societies a murderer may successfully avoid punishment if he leaves the tribe until the outcry and the demand for punishment against him has died down. He may later return and resume his former place in the tribe.

Among the Australian aborigines should a man of one

tribe kill a man of another tribe, reparation must be made, and the reparation is likely to take the following form. The males of the one tribe line up opposite the males of the other tribe, and one by one they begin throwing spears at each other; as soon as the first man is hit—and they take great care not to hit him in any vital part—the match is at an end, and the successful thrower of the spear is required to compensate the family of the injured man. Quarrels between tribes are likely to be settled in a similar manner, but more often by a *corroborree*—a meeting of the tribes to discuss their differences and celebrate their agreements.

WAR

Warfare is completely unknown among the Australian aborigines. The nearest they ever get to anything resembling organized violence is the spear-throwing duel I have described, and this can scarcely be regarded as war. In fact, it is difficult to convince an Australian aboriginal that there are peoples who make organized attacks upon other peoples in order to kill and maim as many of them as possible as quickly as possible. The Eskimos are similarly unacquainted with war as a social activity, and it is equally difficult to convince them that other peoples practice it. The Veddahs of Ceylon are another example of such a people, and so are the Bushman-Hottentots of South Africa. Interestingly enough, all these are food-gathering and hunting peoples and are non-agricultural. Warfare becomes a form of organized activity only at more complex levels of social and technical development. It is among agricultural and pastoral peoples that raiding first begins and becomes increasingly more organized with the increase in economic complexity of societies.

TRESPASSING

Property and, therefore, tribal territory rights are jealously guarded, and in many societies it is considered perfectly justifiable to kill the member of another tribe who has wandered into the tribal territory of another group. In nonliterate societies, taking the life of the member of another tribe is usually not regarded with anything like the same seriousness as murder; in fact, killing a member of another tribe is usually not considered murder and may even be socially sanctioned and encouraged, as among the head-hunting tribes of Borneo, New Guinea, and South America.

SANCTIONED TAKING OF LIFE

Under special but recurring prevalent circumstances in non-literate societies, even the life of a member of the tribe may be taken with the blessing of the tribe. For example, among the Eskimos a member of the group who continues to be particularly difficult and socially disoperative may, by common agreement of the group, be killed. This is usually done with the kindliest of intentions, and the death is made as sudden and as painless as possible. Among the Eskimo, the South African Bushman, and the Australian aborigines, old people who have become helpless and useless will either be abandoned or killed, and this will often be done at their own request.

Among the Australian aborigines a newborn baby will be buried alive or exposed should it be born to a mother who already has a one-year-old and perhaps one or two other children. This is done because it is believed that a newborn baby is not, in fact, quite human, and so a human life is not really being taken and because it is not fair to the older children to have too many young children since the mother cannot pay proper attention to them but must thin it out and share it with too many children. Bringing up human beings, the Australian aborigines hold, is a full-time job. Infanticide is practiced for similar reasons among many other tribes.

SUICIDE

Suicide is not necessarily regarded as self-murder, and in many nonliterate societies there are no penalties whatsoever attaching to such an attempted or successful act. Suicide in some parts of Polynesia, Melanesia, and in other parts of the world, particularly in literate Japan, is often a socially sanctioned practice, either as a face-saving device or as a shaming one. In Japan an impossible situation may be saved by committing hara-kiri, and in some parts of Polynesia and Melanesia one may put one's lover to shame for his fickleness by jumping off the highest palm tree.

RESPECT FOR THE DEAD

In whatever manner they may have died, respect for one's own dead is well-nigh universal, but respect for the dead of another group is by no means universal. There are innumerable peoples who are utterly indifferent to the dead of other peoples, although there are some who pay more elaborate attention to the dead of their enemies than they do to their own. With respect for the dead go more or less elaborate funerary rites and mourning ceremonies. Among some peoples the wives of the dead are required to lacerate themselves and cut off their hair, to anoint themselves with dirt, and maintain a prolonged mourning period; among other peoples, some highly literate like the Hindus, the wives were required to kill themselves. Among the ancient Egyptians slaves were sacrificed and buried with their masters and mistresses, and among many Indian tribes, mostly now extinct, wives were sacrificed at the death of their husbands.

Among the Trobriand Islanders, a year after his father's death a son was supposed to dig up his father's body and procure the forearm bone, upon which he was required to chew periodically.

CANNIBALISM

There are no peoples who have ever made other people a staple article of their diet. In fact, cannibalism (especially eating members of one's own tribe) is more or less strongly discouraged in all human societies, except on certain cere-monial occasions. Not that there exists the slightest evidence of an "instinctive revulsion" against eating human flesh. There does exist no evidence of habitual cannibals. There have been reports of individuals and even of tribes who have enjoyed human flesh, and it is quite probable that could they have obtained a continuous supply they would have made it a staple part of their diet. But the fact is that this has simply not been possible. The following forms of canni-balism may be recognized: *burial cannibalism*, the ceremonial eating of a bit of a dead member of the group, often in order to acquire part of his spirit; *ceremonial cannibalism*, eating part of the body of a slain member of another tribe in order to transfer some of his strength to the consumer; *gastronomic cannibalism*, supplementing one's diet with human flesh as the result of an acquired taste for it; *revenge cannibalism*, eating the flesh of dead enemies as a revenge upon their spirits and as a mark of contempt for them individually; *ritual cannibalism*, eating part of the dead body as part of the ritual solemnizing the departure of a member of the tribe (such ritual cannibalism is usually performed by close relatives); *starvation cannibalism,* under conditions of famine or starvation all peoples have been known to eat their own dead.

Treatment of enemies has varied with different peoples, but among nonliterate peoples generally, the men were usually killed, and sometimes, depending upon circumstances, the women and children were, although more often than not they would be enslaved. Among many Indian tribes the prisoners were systematically tortured, burned at the stake, and their corpses mutilated.

In nonliterate societies the place occupied by the person is not so much dependent upon some abstract valuation of the right of the individual, but rather upon his status as a member of a class, sex, or family. His status determines the roles he plays in his society, whom and when he can marry, what obligations he has to others, and what he may expect from them. This is not to say that his natural or acquired abilities are disregarded; they are not, but in many societies the power of status may loom so large that they may receive very little attention indeed. In some societies, admission to the council of the leaders of the tribe may be achieved only through power and influence when a certain age has been reached. In other societies, it matters not how old the individual may be; if he lacks the necessary wisdom he will not be admitted as a member of the council. On the other hand a young man who has exhibited the requisite wisdom will be so admitted, as among the Australian aborigines.

In all societies skill and ability are admired even though they may often not be rewarded with anything more than admiration. As a rule, the economically more complex societies place increasingly higher valuations upon the artist, the artisan, and the person with special skills, but the rewards may take an almost infinite variety of forms. In many cultures the reward takes the form of an elevation in status. With elevation in status usually go certain perquisites.

All nonliterate societies may, therefore, be said to pay some attention to the individual, the individual not being simply lost in a sea of anonymous persons. The individual is recognized as such, and so are his rights and obligations. But in nonliterate societies somewhat more emphasis is placed upon his roles, not so much as an individual but as the dynamic expression of his status or statuses. Even this is to oversimplify the facts; in any event, in comparison with more highly civilized societies, the rights of the individual as such are not as sharply or as fully realized in nonliterate societies.

In all nonliterate societies children are highly valued, and in most the parents are regarded as responsible for their education and training. Parents who fail to give their children adequate education and training are the subject of a withering public opinion, which renders lapses from the rule rather unusual. There are some societies in which the grandparents, not the parents, are responsible for the raising of the children, but these are exceptional.

Usually the biological family prevails in nonliterate societies, being composed of the biological mother and father and their children. Most societies are patriarchal and patri-lineal and patrilocal; there are some that are matrilineal and matrilocal. In the former, polygyny may be practiced, but usually only a few men have more than one wife. In some matrilineally organized tribes, polyandry may be practiced; here, too, it is usually the case that relatively few women have more than one husband. Where monogamy is the rule, plural marriage is against the law. Divorce exists in all societies and is made more or less difficult. In some societies it is sufficient for one of the partners to declare that the marriage is at an end; in others, the bride price or some other compensation must be made to the spouse's parents. Marriage in some societies is merely a matter of a couple setting up a menage without any formal ceremony whatsoever, as among the Kaingang of South America, and the marriage may be as easily dissolved. Children born out of wedlock may or may not be considered a social embarrassment, but in most nonliterate societies it is considered that every child must have a social father, and even though he may not be the biological father the fiction is often maintained that the male to whom the mother is married is in fact the father.

Incest regulations are universal, though among the kings of ancient Egypt marriage with their sisters was for a time the rule. In some tribes persons will be included in the incest rules who are classificatory but not biological relatives; for example, among the Australian aborigines it is not permitted to marry anyone who is of one's own totemic clan or who stands in certain other classificatory relationships to oneself.

Adultery in some tribes is not considered a serious offense, while in others it may be automatically punishable by death. Among the Eskimos, Australian aborigines, Tahitians, and other peoples, wife lending is considered an obligation of hospitality.

Marriage in some societies entails long-term service obligations to the wife's family, and in others the payment of a bride price, while in still others, no such obligations are entailed. In most nonliterate societies, avoidance of the husband's mother-in-law, by the husband, is the rule. Endogamy is preferred by some tribes, while exogamy is customary in others. In matrilineal societies, as a rule, it is the mother's brother who plays the part of the social father, while the children's own biological father assumes the role in relation to his own sister's children. In many African tribes filial inheritance prescribes that a son will inherit all his father's wives with the exception of his own mother. Sororal polygyny, marriage to one's wife's sisters, is a widespread practice. In many Indian tribes upon marriage a man establishes a lien upon his wife's younger sisters or kinswomen, consummating marriage with them as soon as they reach maturity. Among the Omaha Indians not only was sororal polygyny practiced, but a man could also marry his wife's paternal aunt or her cross-niece, that is, her brother's daughter.

PROPERTY

Attitudes toward property vary among nonliterate peoples, but contrary to certain erroneous beliefs about primitive communism, private property is universally respected. Individual rights in property exist in all nonliterate societies, in property that is real, property that is movable, and property that is incorporeal such as songs, ballads, myths, designs, and the like. It is true, however, that in most nonliterate societies property is more freely shared than in civilized societies. In nonliterate societies property is shared with the members of the group much as it is shared with the members of one's immediate family in our own society. Food is usually shared with everyone and hospitality in such matters is usually carried far beyond the practices customary among civilized peoples. No one in a nonliterate society, not even the laziest ne'er-do-well, need want for food. Such cooperation is considered a moral obligation. Legal or moralistic obligations make it necessary for an aboriginal Australian hunter to desist from consuming any part of the kill until he has distributed its best parts to the other members of his group in a specified order, the older men and women receiving the most desirable portions, and the hunter at last receiving far from the best.

The Caribou Eskimo allow anyone to hunt over their territory in any manner they please; lost property may be retained by the finder, and objects that have been borrowed and then broken or lost need not be replaced by the borrower. Nevertheless, individual property rights are thoroughly respected, and within the same household a kayak may belong to the husband, a mat to the wife, a pot to this child, and a stool to the other, and even the consent of the children must be obtained should a sale of their possessions be considered. Among hunting and herding peoples the ownership of the land is usually shared, that is, it is in the hands of a family hunting band, a clan, or a tribe. Any portion of land, however, in agricultural communities is considered to be owned by its utilizer. Title to land thus rests on use. In many nonliterate societies ownership of the land ceases when failure is made to cultivate it after a varying period of time. A tree planted on the land of another belongs to the planter and not to the owner or cultivator of the land (coconut trees in Polynesia, mango trees, lemon, and other trees in Mexico, palm trees in Africa, and maple trees among the Ojibwa of the Eastern Woodland area); access to the trees must be freely granted by the cultivator of the land.

Property rights in persons, such as slaves, have varied in different nonliterate societies, but as a rule these rights have been quite severely limited, and the most frequent manner in which chattel slavery originates is in the inability of men to pay their debts, who then surrender themselves or their wives or children to the creditor, until by their labor thus pawned the debt is discharged (Northwest California, West Africa). In general in nonliterate societies slaves are treated as members of the family. Children taken in raids are made members of the family and are brought up as members of the tribe with all the rights and privileges of a full member.

In many nonliterate societies the head of the family has the power of life and death over its members (Barea and Kunama of Africa), and in general he may sell any member of the family at will (Bangala, Kimbunda of Africa).

Incorporeal or intangible property even to the extent of skills, such as ironworking, smelting, and the like, are thoroughly respected, and no one will venture to embark upon these occupations without obtaining the permission of the owners of these skills, no more than they would venture to sing the song owned by another without his permission.

Among many California Indians property is not transmitted to one's descendants but is completely destroyed at death. The Ona Indians of Tierra del Fuego wrap up a dead man in his clothes for burial and then put the flame to his hut and all his belongings; only the dogs are turned over to his kinsmen.

Extreme primogeniture as to inheritance is the exception rather than the rule among nonliterate peoples, the eldest son assuming the role of administrator or trustee rather than principal or sole heir. Among some Kirghiz and some Eskimo tribes ultimogeniture or junior right prevails; that is, the youngest son is principal heir.

Correlated with the emphasis among nonliterate peoples on status is the fact that individuals are rarely free to will their property as they choose; inheritance is determined by the social mores.

Attitudes toward women differ, but it requires to be said that the notion that in nonliterate societies women are regarded as little more than beasts of burden or as purely economic assets is far from the truth. In all nonliterate societies the roles of the sexes are distinguished, and it is doubtful whether there are any in which women are not regarded as inferior to men, and this in matrilineal as well as in patrilineal societies. It is extremely rare for women to be admitted to the council of the elders, and women are practically everywhere excluded from the mysteries and professions that are the prerogatives of men. Even cannibalistic activities are restricted to men, and women are usually deprived of participation in such esoteric activities.

It is clear, then, that every society has developed a set of values regulating conduct. The basic themes around which ethical prescriptions have been evolved are universally the same. However, the specific rules in which those prescriptions are codified are as varied and as numerous as the peoples who live by them.

CHAPTER 8

The Biosocial Nature of Man

ARISTOTLE DESCRIBED man as a political animal, thus hitting off in a phrase his essential characteristics, namely, that he is at once an animal and a social creature in a very special sense. All animals are social creatures, but man as an animal and as a social creature is unique in several respects. As an animal man is the most educable, the most plastic of all creatures, and as a social organism man is the most complexly developed of all social organisms. In fact, the difference that characterizes the kind of societies peculiar to nonhuman animals from that characteristic of human social life is so great that it must be considered one of kind rather than of degree of development. The failure to recognize this fact has led to much confusion in discussions of the biosocial nature of man. This confusion, in the recent history of world civilization, has had most disastrous effects.

Theories spun by men desirous of rationalizing their conduct toward other men and discussions of the nature of man in the academies did not remain long in the places of private discourse, for what affects the lives of men sufficiently to become a subject of discourse is likely to become a matter of public interest as soon as the social conditions are favorable. What men understand to be the nature of man appears to determine their attitudes of conduct toward men. The conditions and motivations that lead them to the views they adopt concerning human nature have not often been the subject of inquiry; yet much inquiry is usually of the first importance in throwing light upon the origin of and reasons for the views held. This is an area of human knowledge in which prejudice and pathological thinking have often befouled and beclouded the issues and have led to the most unfortunate social and biological effects. One has but to be reminded of the political enthronement of the doctrine of racism by the Nazis and the consequences of this for millions of human beings, as well as for civilization, to understand how important it is for human beings to become acquainted with the true facts concerning the biosocial nature of man.

In the present chapter we shall be concerned with a critical evaluation of the literature on the biosocial nature of man as reflected in the writings of representative thinkers who have had or may have a considerable influence upon the thought of their contemporaries and upon the development of civilization in the recent past and in the future. This chapter is not a history of theories concerning the biosocial nature of man from antiquity to the present time, but rather it is an evaluation from the standpoint of world history of those theories of the biosocial nature of man that have played an important part in the development of Western civilization or could do so if they were taken seriously enough. Before we pass on to the discussion of modern theories relating to the biosocial nature of man, a few words should be said concerning such theories in antiquity.

THEORIES OF THE BIOSOCIAL NATURE
OF MAN IN ANTIQUITY

The ancient Greeks were monogenists, that is to say, they believed in the descent of all human beings from a common stock.[1] Differences between men, they believed, were largely due to environment. When, in the fourth century, the institution of slavery began increasingly to come under attack, it fell to the lot of Aristotle to develop the necessary theoretical bases upon which to justify its existence. In the *Politics* Aristotle argued that the slave was but a partial man, lacking the governing element of the soul and therefore needing to be ruled by those possessing this element. Some men were more fit by nature to be slaves than were others.[2]

Before Aristotle, Plato had deliberately proposed a piece of disingenuous fiction concerning the innate differences existing between men, calculated to convince the workers that there are people who by nature are better qualified to rule than they.[3] But this "Phoenician Lie," as Plato called it, failed to germinate. Most serious scholars are agreed that, with the exception of Aristotle, while the Greeks affected to despise the barbarian, they did so on purely cultural grounds, never on biological ones.[4] The Greeks, indeed, as Isocrates (436–338 B.C.) put it, thought of Hellenism as a thing of the spirit rather than of race. "So far," he wrote, "has Athens distanced the rest of mankind in thought and in speech that her pupils have become the teachers of the rest of the world; and she has brought it about that the name of 'Hellenes' is applied rather to those who share our culture than to those who share a common blood."[5]

What a people thinks of the biosocial nature of man is reflected in their views on "race." The Greeks, as also the

Romans, were singularly free of anything resembling race prejudice.[6]

A study of the cultures and literatures of mankind, both ancient and recent, shows us that the conception that there are significant, innately determined, mental and biological differences between groups of mankind is an idea that was not developed until the latter part of the eighteenth century.

THE INSTITUTION OF SLAVERY AND THE BIOSOCIAL NATURE OF MAN

The French Revolution may not have succeeded in establishing the principle in the minds of men that liberty, fraternity, and equality constitute a sound doctrine by which to live, but it did at least raise the question in the minds of many who would not otherwise have considered it. The history of the last 180 years could illuminatingly be written in terms of the clash between those who have attempted to implement this doctrine as a way of life, and those who have attempted to tear it down. It is one of the strange twists of history that the land in which the greatest antagonism to that doctrine should have appeared is the United States of America. As a doctrine to which to pay lip-service, the principles of the American Revolution were acceptable enough, but when it came to the question of putting them into practice, 30 per cent profit on each slave stood in the way. When, toward the end of the eighteenth century, voices began to make themselves heard against the inhuman traffic in slaves, and when these voices issued from influential men and organizations, the supporters of slavery, put on the defensive, were forced to look for reasons of a new kind to controvert the dangerous arguments of their opponents. The abolitionists argued that those who were enslaved were as good human beings as those who had enslaved them. To this, by way of reply, the champions of slavery could only attempt to show that the slaves were certainly not as good as their masters. And in this highly charged emotional atmosphere there began the doleful recital of the catalogue of differences, which were alleged to prove the inferiority of the slave to his master.[7]

It is not commonly realized how greatly so many of the biosocial theories of the nature of man have been influenced by the debates that raged over slavery during the period 1775–1870. One side claimed that there were groups of men characterized by physical *and* mental differences who stood lower in the scale of development than other groups; it was also claimed that such differences characterized the different classes of men living in the same society or nation. The other side claimed that apart from physical differences, so far as the races of mankind were concerned, the mental differences that existed between groups of mankind were probably due to differences in opportunity for mental development and that so far as class differences are concerned, mental and even physical differences could be traced to differences in socioeconomic conditions and opportunities for education. The debate still goes on. It received a new accretion of strength with the advent of the Darwinian theory of evolution, in the burgeoning age of the industrial revolution, accompanied by a galloping imperialism and the rising tide of nationalism. It is at this juncture that we may profitably turn to a consideration of the various biosocial theories of the nature of man.

THE DARWINIAN THEORY OF EVOLUTION AND THE BIOSOCIAL NATURE OF MAN

Darwin's great book, published November 24, 1859, was entitled *On the Origin of Species by Means of Natural Selection, Or the Preservation of Favoured Races in the Struggle for Existence*. Here, at once, in the title of this famous and influential book, we perceive that it was taken for granted that some races will be favored in the struggle for existence while others will not. Those who have the necessary adaptive fitness will survive, those who do not will tend to leave a smaller progeny behind them and may even die out.

We know how well this doctrine fit the book of *laissez-faire* capitalism. Here full blown was the scientific validation of the class structure of society and the imperialist, exploitative, endeavors of such a society. It was not, in fact, until 1871, when Darwin published *The Descent of Man*, that what was implicit in the *Origin* was made fully explicit for man:

> Man, like every other animal, has no doubt advanced to his present high condition through a struggle for existence consequent on his rapid multiplication; and if he is to advance still higher, it is to be feared that he must remain subject to a severe struggle. Otherwise he would sink into indolence, and the more gifted men would not be more successful in the battle of life than the less gifted. Hence, our natural rate of increase, though leading to many and obvious evils, must not be greatly diminished by any means. There should be open competition for all men.[8]

The implication here is that man is a naturally competitive creature who has reached his present high condition through competition, and if he is to make any progress, he must continue to compete.

Now, this viewpoint that man is naturally aggressive was by no means new with Charles Darwin; the origin of this viewpoint is lost in the mists of antiquity. What Darwin did was to give it scientific validation. Man, in common with the rest of the animal kingdom, is naturally aggressive, but though that may be natural, Darwin adds:

> Important as the struggle for existence has been and even still is, yet as far as the highest part of man's nature is concerned there are other agencies more important. For the moral qualities are advanced, either directly or indirectly, much more through the effects of habit, the reasoning powers, instruction, religion, &c., than through natural selection.[9]

However, it is quite clear from Darwin's standpoint that the allegedly innate aggressive impulses of man are in conflict with his moral strivings. Now it is not only a highly questionable theory that man is innately aggressive, but there is, indeed, very good reason to believe that the contrary is true.[10] Darwin and the Darwinists, in the spirit of their times, gave too much emphasis to competition as a factor of evolution and not enough to the factor of cooperation.[11] Darwin paid so little attention to the factor of cooperation in the evolution of man that he altogether failed to notice that the effects of good habits, reasoning powers, instruction, and religion, insofar as they confer survival benefits upon human beings, have high natural selective value. As Haldane has pointed out, "in so far as it makes for the survival of one's descendants and near relations, altruistic behavior is a kind of Darwinian fitness, and may be expected to spread as a result of natural selection."[12]

The Darwinian view of man's nature became generalized in the following form: Since man is descended from lower animals and his morphological relationship to those animals can be demonstrated by any competent anatomist, it is evident that man carries within the structure of his inherited dispositions the marks of his lowly ancestry. Competitiveness and aggressiveness are inborn traits of man, so runs this theory, and they cannot be eradicated; the problem is to control them. From Darwin to Freud this is the theme song of innumerable writers, ranging all the way from animalculists to zoologists, and embracing military men, emperors, sociologists, businessmen, politicians, literary critics, musicians, and the man on the street, not to mention practically every other class of human being.

From such a Darwinian standpoint everything from discrimination against persons on the basis of some group membership fancied to be "inferior" to the justification of war, from the conduct of business to the bringing up of children, has been attempted. Darwin's statement that "At some future period, not very distant as measured by centuries, the civilised races of man will almost certainly terminate, and replace, the savage races throughout the world,"[13] was echoed by innumerable thinkers: Ernst Haeckel in Germany and the German general staff, Francis Galton, Karl Pearson, Herbert Spencer, Sir Arthur Keith, and many others in England, and C. B. Davenport, E. M. East, and William McDougall in the United States, and numerous others.[14]

On the whole, the nineteenth century had come to the conclusion that human nature differs racially, ethnically, nationally, and even among social classes of the same people and that these differences are biologically determined. Hence, it became a simple matter to account for the differences in human nature and their cultural expression. Since the differences in human nature were considered to be biologically determined, it became evident that the peoples who had conquered others during the history of the world were superior to those whom they had defeated, and world history could be regarded as a continuation of natural history. It has already been pointed out that this conception of human nature gained ascendancy in the nineteenth century with the rise (in the midst of the industrial revolution and rampant imperialism) of the Darwinian theory of evolution and its doctrine of natural selection, the "struggle for existence," and the "survival of the fittest." Intellectually honest men and distinguished scientists could persuade themselves and others that the virtual enslavement of "the lower classes," the exploitation of the lands of "inferior peoples" and their eventual supplantation by the "white race" were not only biologically justifiable, but the clear judgment of Nature (with a capital N).

Galton held that the quality of a civilization was dependent upon the qualities of the individuals composing it and that the rise and decline of civilizations were associated with the rise and decline of the innate qualities of peoples. Galton took a pessimistic view of man's capacity to maintain civilization at a high level—unless man consciously took into his own hands the matter of securing the persistence of individuals with the highly developed necessary innate qualities. Man, he suggested, could take the breeding of man in hand. Toward this end he proposed (in *Inquiries into Human Faculty and Its Development*, 1883) a science of "eugenics," which he defined as "the science of improving stock, which is by no means confined to questions of judicious mating but which, especially in the case of man, takes cognizance of all influences that end in however remote a degree to give to the more suitable races or strains of blood a better chance of prevailing speedily over the less suitable than they otherwise would have had." Perceive how such a view of human nature leads to racism and the justification of war. Nowhere is this made more explicit than in the famous lecture by Karl Pearson, Galton's friend and pupil, entitled *National Life from the Standpoint of Science* (1901). Pearson writes:

> You will see that my view—and I think it may be called the scientific view of a nation—is that of an organized whole, kept up to a high pitch of internal efficiency by insuring that its numbers are substantially recruited from the better stocks, and kept up to a high pitch of external efficiency by contest, chiefly by way of war with inferior races, and with equal races by the struggle for trade-routes and the sources of raw material and of food supply. This is the natural history view of mankind, and I do not think you can in its main features subvert it.

In yet another famous lecture, this time by Sir Arthur Keith, *The Place of Prejudice in Modern Civilization,* the basic aggressiveness of man is stated for all clearly to read. "Prejudices," Keith writes, "are inborn; are part of the birthright of every child." These prejudices

> have been grafted in our natures for a special purpose—an evolutionary purpose. . . . They are essential parts of the evolutionary machinery which Nature employed throughout eons of time to secure the separation of man into permanent groups and thus to attain production of new and improved races of Mankind. . . . Nature endowed her tribal teams with this spirit of antagonism for her own purposes. It has come down to us and creeps out from our modern life in many shapes, as national rivalries and jealousies and as racial hatreds. The modern name for this spirit of antagonism is race-prejudice. . . . Nature throughout the past has demanded that a people who seeks independence as well as peace can obtain these privileges only in one way—by being prepared to sacrifice their blood to secure them. Nature

keeps her orchard healthy by pruning; war is her pruning hook. We cannot dispense with her services.

These ideas were later repeated by Keith in several articles and two books.

So much for a certain widespread and influential anthropological viewpoint, *physical* anthropological viewpoint, rather than that of the cultural anthropological viewpoint, which, as we shall see, is different.

Even more influential than these viewpoints is that represented by Freud. The Freudian conception of human nature has enjoyed a widespread and pervasive influence. Freud assumes the existence of two basic instincts, Eros and the destructive instinct: "The aim of the first of these basic instincts . . . is to bind together; the aim of the second . . . is to undo connections and so to destroy things. We may suppose that the final aim of the destructive instinct is to reduce living things to an inorganic state. For this reason we also call it the *death instinct.*"[15]

Throughout the writings of Freud the aggressive instinct plays an important role. We are told that "The holding back of aggressiveness is in general unhealthy and leads to illness."[16] Freud always speaks of the "hostile impulses of mankind" as if they were biologically inherited entities, and when he speaks of human culture he says "one gets the impression that culture is something which was imposed on a resisting majority by a minority that understood how to possess itself of the means of power and coercion."[17] Freud's conception of the cyclopean family (in *Totem and Tabu*, 1913), in which the father drives out his sons; his development of the theory of the Oedipus complex, in which it is postulated that as a normal part of the development of every male child, there occurs a consuming jealousy of the father's possession of the child's mother; the concept of narcissism as a stage of self-love in the development of every infant; and many similar notions were instrumental in conveying a picture of the biosocial nature of man as an essentially selfish, aggressive creature, driven by blind creative and destructive forces, which it was doubtful that man could successfully control.[18] This view of man's nature has colored much of the thinking of innumerable workers in the social and psychological sciences. Let me quote one example from a psychoanalytic writer who belongs to the school of Jung, Dr. M. E. Harding. Harding writes:

> Beneath the decent façade of consciousness with its disciplined, moral order and its good intentions, lurk the crude instinctive forces of life, like monsters of the deep—devouring, begetting, warring endlessly. They are for the most part unseen, yet on their urge and energy life itself depends: without them human beings would be as inert as stones. But were they left to function unchecked, life would lose its meaning, being reduced once more to mere birth and death, as in the teeming world of the primordial swamps. In creating civilization man sought, however unconsciously, to curb these natural forces and to channel some part at least of their energy into forms that would serve a different purpose. For with the coming of consciousness, cultural and psychological values began to compete with the purely biological aims of unconscious functioning.[19]

This is a typical utterance of the Freudian and the Jungian schools of psychoanalysis on the biosocial nature of man. Alfred Adler takes a very different view of man's nature. "The growing, irresistible evolutionary advance of social feeling," he writes, "warrants us in assuming that the existence of humanity is inseparably bound up with 'goodness.' Anything that contradicts this is to be considered as a failure in evolution; it can be traced back to mistakes that have been made . . . to a failure, however produced, in one's growth in social feeling."[20]

Ian Suttie, in what is undoubtedly the most original, profoundest, and most sympathetic of the critiques of Freud, *The Origins of Love and Hate* (1939), finds Freud's view of the biosocial nature of man utterly unacceptable and not in agreement with the facts; he anticipates Adler in showing that the human being's great biological need is for sociability and *not* for a combination of destructiveness and love. Freud's view of human nature conceives of man as born with a turmoil of energies, the id, which provides the source of the energies out of which the ego is in part developed, the ego always retaining its roots in the id and also deriving part of its energy from various organs and parts of the body. But the struggle between Eros and Thanatos, the binding-together instinct and the death instinct, is always paramount. "One has to reckon," says Freud, "with the fact that there are present in all men destructive, and therefore anti-social and anti-cultural tendencies, and that with a great number of people these are strong enough to determine their behavior in human society." Hence, it seems probable to Freud that "every culture must be built upon coercion and instinctual renunciation; it does not even appear certain that without coercion the majority of human individuals would be ready to submit to the labour necessary for acquiring new means of supporting life."[21]

Freud's view of man was a deeply pessimistic one, and this pessimism increased as he grew older. An examination of Freud's own life shows us that he was as much a child of his time as we are of ours. Growing up in nineteenth-century Vienna, in a patriarchal family, discriminated against because he was Jewish, struggling for existence in a highly competitive society, Freud fully absorbed the Darwinian viewpoint and the conception of man as a brute struggling to be free of his destructive impulses but failing most of the time. That the idea of a death instinct should appeal to such a thinker, even though the biology it is based on is demonstrably unsound, that psychoanalysis should develop into a theory of behavior without women and without love, would almost have been predictable in terms of Freud's own life.[22] Psychoanalytic theory, as distinct from psychoanalytic practice, constitutes a reflection of Freud's own acquired nature.

The evidence concerning the biosocial nature of man as we know it today may be summarized as follows. The organism *Homo sapiens* is born the most plastic, the most educable of all living things.[23] But it is not born the undifferentiated behavioral creature that has long been thought, for already *in utero* it is capable of experiencing and responding to a large variety of different stimuli, which may leave a deep impress upon it.[24] It is now known that an emotionally disturbed pregnant woman may measurably affect the behavior of the fetus, to the extent of producing a neurotic child at birth.[25] Until recently it was believed that there was no nervous connection between the mother and the fetus. This is now known to be wrong. There is a very intimate nervous connection between mother and fetus through the agency of the neurohumoral system, that is, the interacting nervous and endocrine systems acting through the fluid medium of the blood and its oxygen and carbon dioxide content. It is now also known that the fetus can be conditioned *in utero*.[26] In any complete view of the biosocial nature of man, these are important facts to take into consideration. We now know that there is more than a modicum of truth in Samuel Taylor Coleridge's remark, "Yes, the history of man for the nine months preceding his birth, would, probably, be far more interesting, and contain events of greater moment than all the threescore and years that follow it."

At birth the child has certain basic needs that must be satisfied if the child is to survive. These needs are oxygen hunger, thirst, sleep, rest, activity, bowel and bladder elimination, avoidance of pain, fear, and sex. Satisfaction of these needs will enable the organism to survive. But survival is a means to an end; it is not an end in itself. It would seem that the function of life is living; the organism that does not enjoy life hardly considers life worth living. What the organism wants is to live a healthy, enjoyable life. It wants to be loved, and it wants to love. If the human organism is not adequately loved, even though all its physical needs are satisfied, it fails to develop as a harmonic, integrated, healthy human being. The most important nourishment the infant and child requires during its development is the feeling that is conveyed to it that it is loved, that there is a person or persons who are profoundly interested in its welfare, who are there to support and encourage it and to give it all the assistance and stimulation it requires. It is now known that failing such experience in love, most children grow up to be "affectionless characters," suffering from affect hunger and exhibiting the privation of love they have suffered in their own inability to love.[27] Such individuals are problem children and problem adults. Not having learned to love by having been loved, they are exceedingly awkward as social human beings and are extremely dependent upon others for love. The social consequences of such personalities are serious, contributing largely to the ranks of juvenile delinquents, criminals, and those seekers after the substitutes for love who, in their quest for power, may come to occupy important and influential positions in their societies and who often, in the course of coming to occupy such positions, and in occupying them, do great social and personal damage.[28] In order to become an adequate, healthy, cooperative, loving human being, it is necessary to be loved. No child is born hostile or aggressive. It becomes so only when its desires to be loved and to love are frustrated, that is, when its expected satisfactions are thwarted. This is what Freud failed to perceive. What he took to be inborn hostility is, in fact, an acquired form of behavior following upon the frustration of one's expected satisfactions. Hostility, aggressiveness, and "bad behavior" are simply techniques for securing love, for compelling the attention of those who have refused it. While the psychophysical mechanism to develop aggressiveness as a result of the thwarting of expected satisfactions is inherited, aggressiveness as such is not inherited. Recent students of infant and child behavior are, for the most part, unanimous in agreeing that children are not born aggressive. Thus, Professor Lauretta Bender, a child psychiatrist, writes that hostility, far from being inborn

> is a symptom complex resulting from deprivations which are caused by developmental discrepancies in the total personality structure such that the constructive patterned drives for action in the child find inadequate means of satisfaction and result in amplification or disorganization of the drives into hostile or destructive aggression. . . . The child acts as though there were an inherent awareness of his needs and there is thus the expectation of having them met. A failure in this regard is a deprivation and leads to frustration and a reactive aggressive response.[29]

Indeed, the developmental directiveness of the organism is toward maturation in terms of cooperation. Bender calls it "the inherent capacity or drive for normality." And she says, "The emphasis on the inborn or instinctive features of hostility, aggression, death wishes, and the negative emotional experiences represents a one-sided approach which has led our students of child psychology astray."

In an important paper, Professor A. H. Maslow has examined the viewpoint that "man's deepest impulses are bad, evil, undesirable, selfish, criminal, or otherwise reprehensible" and has found it completely wanting. Professor Maslow writes:

> I find children, up to the time they are spoiled and flattened out by the culture, nicer, better, more attractive human beings than their elders, even though they are of course more "primitive" than their elders. The "taming and transforming" that they undergo seems to hurt rather than help. It was not for nothing that a famous psychologist once defined adults as "deteriorated children."[30]

Professor Maslow puts the modern viewpoint neatly:

> Those human impulses which have seemed throughout our history to be deepest, to be most instinctive and unchangeable, to be mostly widely spread throughout mankind, *i.e.*, the impulses to hate, to be jealous, to be hostile, to be greedy, to be egoistic and selfish, are now being discovered more and more clearly to be acquired and *not* instinctive. They are almost certainly neurotic and sick reactions to bad situations, more specifically to frustrations of our truly basic and instinct-like needs and impulses.[31]

This essentially represents the viewpoint of such psychoanalysts as Karen Horney, Erich Fromm, Harry Stack Sullivan, and others.[32] It is a different viewpoint from that represented by Freud. Far from man's being born aggressive and hostile and therefore having to be disciplined into being "good," the evidence strongly indicates that man is born quite the opposite, namely, cooperative and desiring to be loved and to love. As Maslow says:

> It looks more and more as if . . . [the] instinct-like impulses have been maligned unjustly; they seem to be good rather than bad, desirable and not undesirable and certainly not intrinsic sources of trouble. See if you think the following to be in themselves the causes of war, murder, and hatred: the needs for safety or security, to love and to be loved, to have a group to belong to, to be respected and appreciated, to have a good opinion of oneself, to develop one's talents, to seek for beauty, to seek for knowledge, and to seek for understanding and wisdom![33]

The evidence strongly suggests that it is no longer true to say that man is born neither good nor evil, but simply indifferent, that what the human organism will become as a human being depends largely upon the kind of experience offered to it. This is, of course, to a great extent true, but what does not appear to be true is that the organism is born indifferent, neither good nor evil, for the facts strongly suggest that the organism is born positively good—good in the sense that it wants to love and to be loved, does not want to injure or to be injured.

The psychobiological benefits that are reciprocally conferred upon each other by mother and child are operative from birth. It is now known that when immediately after birth the child is left in contact with the mother, certain physiological changes biologically advantageous to each of them occur in both of them—changes that would not occur were child and mother to be separated from one another. In the mother the uterus tends to undergo contraction and return to a normal size much more rapidly than is ever the case when the child is removed from the mother; also bleeding from the uterus is greatly reduced. These changes are accelerated when the baby is put to nurse at the mother's breast. The baby, in turn, begins to breathe much more efficiently, and its alimentary tract works more efficiently. There can be little doubt that the psychic benefits are equally great.

We see here, then, how from the very outset interrelatedness confers survival benefits upon the interacting organisms; it is interrelatedness that the organism strives to maintain, and any interference with that state, howsoever it may have come about, constitutes an interference with the healthy development of the organism. The evidence indicates beyond any shadow of doubt that all human beings everywhere are similarly constituted in their desire to love and be loved. There is no evidence whatever that human beings are born with any individual or group antagonisms whatever. Human nature is fundamentally everywhere the same; it is only its secondary or cultural expression that differs.

There is a tendency to confuse what is culturally acquired and becomes habitual, that is, *second nature*, with what is taken to be inborn, that is, *primary nature*. Yet the term "second nature" is a recognition both of the acquired character of what it refers to and also of the possibility of confusion with "primary nature." It may be said that the relevant research of this century points to the fact that all behavior that exhibits a cultural quality is learned behavior and that practically all the cultural behavior of a human being is of this nature. Such behavior is acquired during the socialization process. When such behavior becomes habitual, it seems "natural," but it is, in fact, only secondarily so and not originally so. Because man makes his own nature, that is to say, has it made for him by other human beings, out of a unique set of potentialities that distinguishes him from all other creatures, it is the greatest folly to assert that human nature cannot be changed. Man is custom made, tailored according to the prevailing cultural pattern into which he is born; as the customs change, so do the patterns and so does the finished product.

Consider, for example, the seafaring Scandinavians of the Bronze Age, undoubtedly the ancestors of the modern Scandinavians: How different is the cultural behavior of the modern, relatively sedentary, Scandinavians from that of their raiding forebears!

The boisterous joy of life of the English of Elizabeth I's time and the lusty libertinism of the Restoration contrast sharply with the prudery of the Victorian Age. The Englishman's "nature" was different in the sixteenth from what it was in the seventeenth century, and it was still more different in the nineteenth century.[34]

With respect to the Germans, it would be difficult to do better than cite the comments of an eighteenth-century Scottish traveler, William Guthrie, who wrote, "The Germans are by nature honest, hospitable people, passionately fond of liberty, and very little versed in dissimulation and artifice. . . . The Germans are brave, and when led by generals, particularly Italians, have often performed great deeds."[35]

"Led by generals, particularly Italians," is a remark that in the light of later German-Italian military relations is quite too piquant and should provide an interesting commentary in itself upon the mutability of human nature.

And what shall we say of the differences in cultural behavior of such biologically near kin as the New Mexican sedentary Pueblo and the nomadic Navaho Indians or the behavior of those inhabitants of Mexican Indian villages who are completely Hispanicized?

What can have happened to the alleged "warlike nature" of the American Indians who today live at peace with their white and Indian "enemies"?

Is the cultural behavior of the Japanese the same as it was a hundred years ago?

Compare the great Polynesian maritime peoples with their descendants today in Hawaii and New Zealand. Biologically they are mostly the same people, but so far as the expression of their "nature" is concerned they are virtually completely Westernized.

The one thing characteristic of human nature is its changeability under changing conditions. The one characteristic of man as man is his ability to make all the necessary changes within himself to meet the demands of a changing environment. This trait, plasticity or educability or adaptability, is the one the human species as a whole has had the greatest demands made upon it by natural and social selection. Survival of the human species and its progress has depended upon the ability of human nature to change in adaptation to changed conditions.

What most people take to be human nature is really second nature, a nature that has been acquired in terms of the potentialities of being human in a specific culture. Human nature is a pattern of behavior, and this pattern of behavior is known to be capable of change not only from generation to generation but in the same person within a single generation.

It is because human nature is often thought to be primary nature when it is in fact second that the facts are reversed and culture is made to be an expression of human nature. Whereas, in fact, human nature is an expression of culture, and in the absence of cultural stimulation the organism *Homo sapiens* simply fails to express any nature at all—apart from the phenomena of purely physical functioning, and even there, in its physical functioning, such an organism remains virtually completely undeveloped.

We arrive at the conclusion then that human nature is learned, acquired within the limits of those uniquely human potentialities for being human in a specific culture or in any culture whatever. It is because no other animal possesses such potentialities that it cannot be taught what human beings are capable of learning. Hence, educability is a species character of *Homo sapiens.*

Human nature does not undergo an automatic predetermined or programed unfolding under the stimulation of the proper conditions; on the contrary, human nature neither unfolds nor automatically develops but is taught, and it is learned according to the ability of the organism and the kind of teaching offered to it. Ability is itself much modified by sociobiologic factors of an external nature, such as socioeconomic status, state of nutrition, health, disease, and psychic well being. What an organism will learn will depend upon all these factors; the kinds of things it learns are determined by the culture or segment thereof in which the organism finds itself, and the nature of that organism will be expressed in terms of the cultural conditioning, the socialization process, which it undergoes in a particular culture. If all human beings were brought up in the same culture, they would exhibit a basic personality structure of the same kind; they would speak a common language; and they would be recognizable as belonging to the same culture. The reason great groups of human beings exist who exhibit different expressions of human nature is not that their basic or primary nature differs but that they exhibit the evidence of a different history of cultural experience, which experience has a long and unique history behind it.

It is not because of any differences in primary nature that

the cultures of the different ethnic groups of man differ so much from one another, but because of the differences in the history of experience each group has undergone. While it is possible to make this statement with a high degree of probability, it should, however, be pointed out that it is only a probability statement, for we are by no means certain that some biogenic differences in potentialities do not exist between some, at any rate, of the ethnic groups of mankind. What we can say is that in spite of all attempts to find such differences, none has been found. As the UNESCO Statement on Race of 1950 puts it:

> It is now generally recognized that intelligence tests do not in themselves enable us to differentiate safely between what is due to innate capacity and what is the result of environmental influences, training, and education. Wherever it has been possible to make allowances for differences in environmental opportunities the tests have shown essential similarity in mental characters among all human groups. In short, given similar degrees of cultural opportunity to realize their potentialities, the average achievement of each ethnic group is about the same. The scientific investigations of recent years fully support the dictum of Confucius (551–478 B.C.) "Men's natures are alike; it is their habits that carry them far apart."

The 1952 UNESCO Statement on the Nature of Race and Race Differences by Physical Anthropologists and Geneticists puts it this way:

> Studies within a single race have shown that both innate capacity and environmental opportunity determine the results of tests of intelligence and temperament, though their relative importance is disputed.

When intelligence tests, even non-verbal, are made on a group of non-literate people, their scores are usually lower than those of more civilized people. It has been recorded that different groups of the same race occupying similarly high levels of civilization may yield considerable differences in intelligence tests. When, however, the two groups have been brought up from childhood in similar environments, the differences are usually very slight. Moreover, there is good evidence that, given similar opportunities, the average performance (that is to say, the performance of the individual who is representative because he is surpassed by as many as he surpasses), and the variation round it, do not differ appreciably from one race to another.

Even those psychologists who claim to have found the greatest differences in intelligence between groups of different racial origin, and have contended that they are hereditary, always report that some members of the group of inferior performance surpass not merely the lowest ranking member of the superior group, but also the average of its members. In any case, it has never been possible to separate members of two groups on the basis of mental capacity, as they can often be separated on a basis of religion, skin colour, hair form or language. It is possible, though not proved, that some types of innate capacity for intellectual and emotional responses are commoner in one human group than in another, but it is certain that, within a single group, innate capacities vary as much as, if not more than, they do between different groups.

. . . The normal individual, irrespective of race, is essentially educable. It follows that his intellectual and moral life is largely conditioned by his training and by his physical and social environment.

It often happens that a national group may appear to be characterized by particular psychological attributes. The superficial view would be that this is due to race. Scientifi·

cally, however, we realize that any common psychological attribute is more likely to be due to a common historical and social background, and that such attribute may obscure the fact that, within different populations consisting of many human types, one will find approximately the same range of temperament and intelligence.

The scientific material available to us at present does not justify the conclusion that inherited genetic differences are a major factor in producing the differences between the cultures and cultural achievements of different peoples or groups. It does indicate, on the contrary, that a major factor in explaining such differences is the cultural experience which each group has undergone.

Most scientists at the present day would subscribe to these conclusions.[36]

The racist viewpoint maintains that there is an indissoluble association or linkage between physical and mental characteristics, that this association is determined by "race," and that this something called "race" is the prime determiner of all the important traits of body and soul, of character and personality, of human beings and of nations. The racists further allege that this something called "race" is a fixed and unchangeable part of the germ plasm, which is transmitted from generation to generation, and unfolds in each people as a typical expression of personality and culture. Associated with the names of Gobineau, Houston Stewart Chamberlain, Richard Wagner, and Adolf Hitler, not to mention hundreds of other lesser luminaries, there exists not the slightest evidence in support of the racist viewpoint.[37] Nevertheless, this viewpoint has had a great influence upon Western civilization. Closely identified in the nineteenth century with the rise of imperialism (if the doctrine had not already existed the imperialists would have invented it[38]), racism gave a biological validation, as it were, to the activities of the imperial-ists. From the exploitation of primitive peoples or "inferior races" in "other" parts of the world, to the "expropriation" of "inferior races" in one's own and in neighboring territories was but a step, the inevitability of which was foreseen by many writers.[39] Enthroned as a political doctrine by Hitler, the tragically disastrous results of this doctrine for the West-ern world are too recent to need further reference here. At the present time, in South Africa, the tradition of racism as a political doctrine is being continued to divide white and black. Clearly, the facts about race as science has revealed them make little impact. Indeed, recent studies have shown that the problem of racism is fundamentally a problem of socialization, a problem of personality development.[40] As Bettelheim and Janowitz put it:

> It seems reasonable to assume that as long as anxiety and insecurity persist as a root of intolerance, the effort to dispel stereotyped thinking or feelings of ethnic hostility by rational propaganda is at best a half-measure. On an indi-vidual level only greater personal integration combined with social and economic security seem to offer hope for better inter-ethnic relations.[41]

The problem of race is essentially a problem of human relations, and until we improve our human relations that prob-lem threatens to remain with us.

A biologistic interpretation of human nature that has in recent years been revived is that of the constitutionalists. This constitutional psychology is in the direct line of descent of Lombroso in that it attempts to show that physical traits and mental traits are significantly related.

Criminals have made a special appeal to constitutionalists because they exhibit what is taken to be an extreme form of human behavior, an anti-social form of behavior that has many categories. Criminals, therefore, lend themselves to constitutional studies in a special manner, for by their anti-social behavior they are presumed to have differentiated themselves from the rest of the population, and hence, if criminals exhibit any special physical traits that do not characterize the law-abiding population either at all or in any such frequencies, we may have here evidence of the constitutional origins of criminal behavior on the one hand and normal behavior on the other.

As far as personality traits of criminals as compared with noncriminals are concerned, it has been shown by Schleussler and Cressey, who examined 113 studies with a view to throwing some light upon this subject, that a series of 113 studies did not provide a consistent demonstration that criminals differ from noncriminals with reference to any personality trait.[42]

In the light of such an analysis as that of Schleussler and Cressey it would be unnecessary to consider the studies they surveyed any further, but reference should be made to one of the most pretentious of these because it so clearly illustrates the faults and the failures of all such studies. I refer to Professor E. A. Hooton's studies.[43]

Hooton's first report is based on the examination of 4,212 native old American prisoners and 313 native white civilians. Unlike Lombroso, Hooton did not set out with any preconceived notions concerning the nature of physical marks of inferiority, but was content to allow the greater frequency with which certain physical characteristics occurred in his criminal series as compared with his civilian series to indicate these. Thus, he writes, "if we find felons who manifest physical differences from civilians, we are justified in judging as undesirable biological characters those which are associated in the organism with anti-social behavior. . . . It is the organic complex which must be estimated inferior or superior on the basis of the type of behavior emanating from such a combination of parts functioning as a unit." Hooton's findings lead him to assert that "whatever the crime may be, it ordinarily arises from a deteriorated organism. . . . You may say that this is tantamount to a declaration that the primary cause of crime is biological inferiority—and that is exactly what I mean."[44] Hooton goes even further and states, "I deem human [biological] deterioration to be ultimately responsible not only for crime, but for the evils of war, the oppression of the populace by totalitarian states, and for all the social cataclysms which are rocking the world and under which civilization is tottering."[45]

An analysis of the characters studied by Hooton in the light of the biological standards of what are generally accepted to be "advanced," "indifferent," and "primitive" human characters yields interesting results. By such standards it is found that Hooton's criminal series show only 4 per cent primitive, 15.8 per cent indifferent, and 49.5 per cent of advanced characters, more frequently than the noncriminal sample!

By biological standards Hooton's criminal series would, on the whole, appear to be superior to his noncriminal series! Whatever such a finding may mean, the fact is that Hooton did not draw his criminal and noncriminal series from the same local, social, economic, and occupational levels of the population, and furthermore, almost half of his check sample was drawn from 146 Nashville firemen—in an occupation for which, Hooton observes, "the physical qualifications are rather stringent."

In order to make any biological test of differential behavior, it is necessary that both the criminal series and the check noncriminal series be in every respect similar except in the one condition of behavior. The two series must be drawn from the same population or populations, from the same areas, and must come from the same social, economic, and occupational levels. When these requirements have been satisfied and a significantly higher frequency of certain physical characteristics is found among the criminals than among the noncriminals, it may legitimately be inferred that there is some significant *association* between criminal behavior and the presence of a high frequency of such characteristics in an individual or in a group. But to infer from this that such characteristics reflect the cause of criminal behavior is to misunderstand the nature of causation.

In his investigation Hooton did not satisfy the requirement of equating the conditions of his two groups in all but those in which they were being compared, and he did fall into the error of taking a statistical association to be a cause.[46]

The fact is that Hooton's work throws no light whatever upon any possible relation between physical characters and criminality.

Another constitutionalist who claims to have found a highly significant correlation between physical characters and criminality is W. H. Sheldon, who is well known for his work on "somatotyping." This is a method, devised by Sheldon, in which human body types are described in terms of their form as endomorphic, mesomorphic, or ectomorphic.[47] Sheldon claims to have found high correlations between these body types and certain forms of temperament. No other investigator has thus far succeeded in corroborating Sheldon's claims. Sheldon set up a series of arbitrary types and attempted to relate certain temperamental traits to those types. Thus far, he has had no more success in doing so than Ernst Kretschmer had in attempting to relate psychiatric disorders to body types.[48] In a later work Sheldon reports a study of two hundred delinquent youths.[49] This work should give the *coup de grace* to Sheldon's whole superstructure of ideas, and since it is a self-administered and unintended *coup*, it should be all the more effective. The work is written in a highly caustic style, with a complete absence of the dispassion and impartiality of the scientist. It is reminiscent of nothing more than the innuendoes of a soothsayer, and in spite of a great show of method and the use of an esoteric jargon all the author's own, the impression the book makes is dismal. One has no idea whether the two hundred youths examined represented a random sample of the institutional population in which they were examined or what that population was supposed to be. Sheldon defines delinquency as "disappointingness," and, as a great American criminologist, Edwin H. Sutherland, has pointed out in a devastating critique of Sheldon's book, "the feelings of Dr. Sheldon are obviously the criterion of disappointingness."[50] On another page Sheldon tells us that "delinquent performance is failure to use religious energy in such a way as to secure, protect, and guide the biological future of the species."[51] This definition makes most people delinquent, and this is exactly what Sheldon says. Sheldon finds that the entire number of criminals in his series, a total of sixteen, are endomorphic mesomorphs. He states that sixteen of the most famous generals in history or vigorously successful businessmen or leading politicians would fall into the same somatotypic classification. To be an endomorphic mesomorph "means energetic vitality and freedom from inhibition, two cardinal factors in success at most of the things men undertake. . . . Two professions which I hope are otherwise unrelated appear especially to call for these qualities. They are professional criminality and the writing of fiction."[52] Sheldon does not suggest that endomorphic mesomorphy "predisposes toward criminality, but it might mean that to make a go of being a criminal requires a certain amount of guts that is usually found only" in this somatotype. This is *precisely* the point. There is a certain amount of social selection at work in criminal as for many other types of social and anti-social activities. Clearly, the robust, big-chested tough-looking male has a great advantage over the roly-poly endomorph or long linear ectomorph if he is to embark upon a criminal career necessitating the use of some strength and even violence. But Sheldon inclines to attribute this selection more to "guts" than to "occupational requirements." In this opinion he stands with Hooton, with whom he identifies himself, virtually alone. What Sheldon really believes about criminals he states quite clearly. "Perhaps," he writes, "the persistently criminal boy is expressing not so much a 'psychogenic resentment against the mother' as a Dionysian reaction which is almost as much a product of his constitutional design as the way he walks."[53] It is quite evident, as one reads Sheldon, that he believes man to be in a state of biological deterioration from which he can be saved only by eugenic planning and that unless this is done civilization is doomed. This is the burden of the last section of *Varieties of Delinquent Youth*. In the last analysis human nature and body type are indissolubly associated, according to Sheldon. Hence, if we are to safeguard our civilization against the wrong body types we ought to have a sort of national registry of body types, so that we could have them under proper control! If anyone thinks that this is the writer's little joke, let me say at once that this is exactly what Sheldon suggests. In *Varieties of Delinquent Youth*, Sheldon writes:

For a fraction of the cost of maintaining the rearguard palliation that we do against cancer, which may be only one kind of hereditary constitutional disease, we could keep central files of standardized photographs of the entire population. Such photographs taken periodically for a half-dozen generations, and accompanied by concise medical and social histories, might accomplish more against the remediable ills that beset human life (including cancer) than would even a first-rate semifinal war against Russia.[54]

The existence of a relationship between constitution and disease is understandable, but the alleged existence of a relationship between constitution and behavior is a matter of a totally different sort. Human behavior is on a very different plane of integration from disease. The one is largely a function of biological factors, the other largely of social learning and experience. Constitutionalists habitually commit the pathetic biologistic error of taking man to be largely a function of his genes and forget altogether that all genes undergo expression as a result of the interaction with and through the alembic of a complex environment.

CONCLUSION

What we as students of man need to understand is that the biosocial nature of man is such that man may be truly described as the most unique of all living creatures because of his possession in so highly developed a degree of the capacity for learning. Indeed, a species characteristic that should be part of the definition of *Homo sapiens* is educability. Man is the most plastic, the most educable, the most malleable of all creatures on the face of the earth—the creature, beyond all others, that makes the reductionist fallacy, which has it that man is "nothing but" a function of his genes, ridiculous. Actually, man is the only creature capable of controlling the expression of his genes through the manipulation of the social environment in which they undergo development. Educability is, in reality, man's most important species trait, overshadowing all others. It, therefore, cannot be too strongly stated that education is the principal means through which we can achieve the realization of man's evolutionary destiny. What that evolutionary destiny is we can already begin dimly to perceive, but at present it looks very much as if it is to live as if to live and love were one.

NOTES

[1] E. E. Sikes, *The Anthropology of the Greeks* (London: David Nutt, 1914).

[2] Aristotle, *Politics*, I. ii. To this Rousseau made an excellent reply: "Aristotle said," he writes, "that men were not naturally equal, but that some were born for slavery, and others for domination. Aristotle was right, but he took the effect for the cause. Nothing can be more certain than that every man born in slavery is born for slavery. Slaves lose all in their chains, even the desire to leave them; they love servitude as the companions of Ulysses loved brutishness. If then, there are slaves by nature, it is because there have been slaves contrary to nature. Force made the first slaves, their cowardice perpetuated them." Rousseau, *The Social Contract*, I. ii.

[3] Plato, *The Republic*, 547a.

[4] R. Schlaifer, "Greek Theories of Slavery from Homer to Aristotle," *Harvard Studies in Classical Philology*, Vol. 47 (1936), pp. 165–204; F. M. Snowden, Jr., *The Negro in Ancient Greece* (Cambridge: Harvard University Press, 1970).

[5] Isocrates, *Panegyricus*, 4, 50.

[6] A. Diller, "Race Mixture Among the Greeks Before Alexander," *Illinois Studies in Language and Literature* (1937); M. P. Nilsson, "The Race Problem of the Roman Empire," *Hereditas*, Vol. 2 (1921),

pp. 370–90; F. G. Detweiler, "The Rise of Modern Race Antagonisms," *American Journal of Sociology*, Vol. 38 (1932), pp. 738–47; M. McClure, "Greek Genius and Race Mixture," *Studies in the History of Ideas*, Vol. 3 (1935), pp. 25–33; T. J. Haarhoff, *Stranger at the Gate* (New York: Macmillan, 1948); S. Davis, *Race Relations in Ancient Egypt* (New York: Philosophical Library, 1951).

⁷ M. F. Ashley Montagu, *Man's Most Dangerous Myth: The Fallacy of Race*, 4th ed. (New York: World, 1964); W. E. Dodd, *The Cotton Kingdom* (New York: Yale University Press, 1919); J. S. Redding, *They Came in Chains* (Philadelphia: Lippincott, 1950); J. H. Franklin, *From Slavery to Freedom* (New York: Knopf, 1947).

⁸ Charles Darwin, *The Descent of Man* (London: John Murray, 1871), Ch. 21.

⁹ *Ibid.*

¹⁰ M. F. Ashley Montagu, *On Being Human*, rev. ed. (New York: Hawthorn Books, 1966).

¹¹ M. F. Ashley Montagu, *Darwin, Competition, and Cooperation* (New York: Schuman, 1952).

¹² J. B. S. Haldane, *The Causes of Evolution* (New York: Longmans, 1935), p. 131.

¹³ Darwin, *The Descent of Man*, Part 1, Ch. 6.

¹⁴ Ernst Haeckel, *Freedom in Science and Teaching* (New York. Appleton, 1879); F. von Bernhardi, *Germany and the Next War* (New York: Longmans, 1911); F. Galton, *Hereditary Genius* (New York: Macmillan, 1869); F. Galton, *Inquiries into Human Faculty and Its Development* (New York: Macmillan, 1883); K. Pearson, *National Life from the Standpoint of Science* (London: Black, 1901); K. Pearson, *The Groundwork of Eugenics* (London: Dulau, 1909); Herbert Spencer, *Principles of Sociology* (New York: Appleton, 1876–80); A. Keith, *The Place of Prejudice in Modern Civilization* (New York: John Day, 1931); A. Keith, *Essays on Human Evolution* (New York: Putnam, 1947); A. Keith, *A New Theory of Human Evolution* (New York: Philosophical Library, 1948); C. B. Davenport, *Heredity in Relation to Eugenics* (New York: Holt, 1911); C. B. Davenport and Morris Steggerda, *Race Crossing in Jamaica* (Washington, D.C.: Carnegie Institution of Washington, 1929); E. M. East, *Mankind at the Crossroads* (New York: Scribner, 1923); E. M. East, *Heredity and Human Affairs* (New York: Scribner, 1927); W. McDougall, *Is America Safe for Democracy?* (New

York: Scribner, 1921); W. McDougall, *Ethics and Some Modern World Problems* (New York: Putnam, 1924).

[15] Sigmund Freud, *An Outline of Psychoanalysis* (New York: Norton, 1949), p. 20.

[16] *Ibid.*, p. 22.

[17] Sigmund Freud, *The Future of an Illusion* (London: Hogarth Press, 1928), p. 10.

[18] See Sigmund Freud, *Beyond the Pleasure Principle* (London: Hogarth Press, 1922); Sigmund Freud, *Civilization and Its Discontents* (London: Hogarth Press, 1929).

[19] M. E. Harding, *Psychic Energy* (New York: Pantheon Books, 1947), p. 1.

[20] Alfred Adler, *Social Interest: A Challenge to Mankind* (New York: Putnam, 1938), p. 48.

[21] *The Future of an Illusion*, p. 11.

[22] See Ian Suttie's admirable analysis of Freud and psychoanalytic theory in such terms in his chapter "Freudian Theory Is Itself a Disease," in *The Origins of Love and Hate* (New York: Julian Press, 1952); see also Helen Walker Puner, *Freud: His Life and His Mind* (New York: Howell, Soskin, 1947); Hanns Sachs, *Freud: Master and Friend* (Cambridge, Mass.: Harvard University Press, 1944).

[23] Th. Dobzhansky and M. F. Ashley Montagu, "Natural Selection and the Mental Capacities of Mankind," *Science*, Vol. 105 (1947), pp. 587–90.

[24] A survey of the evidence will be found in M. F. Ashley Montagu, *Prenatal Influences* (Springfield, Ill.: Charles C. Thomas, 1962; M. F. Ashley Montagu, *Life Before Birth* (New York: New American Library, 1965).

[25] L. W. Sontag, "The Significance of Fetal Environmental Differences," *American Journal of Obstetrics and Gynecology*, Vol. 42 (1941), pp. 996–1003; L. W. Sontag, "Differences in Modifiability of Fetal Behavior and Physiology," *Psychosomatic Medicine*, Vol. 6 (1944), pp. 151–54.

[26] D. K. Spelt, "The Conditioning of the Human Fetus *in Utero*," *Journal of Experimental Psychology*, Vol. 38 (1948), pp. 338–46.

[27] For a full and authoritative survey of the evidence see John Bowlby, *Maternal Care and Mental Health* (Geneva: World Health Organization, 1951).

[28] See Alfred Adler, *Social Interest: A Challenge to Mankind;* M. F. Ashley Montagu, *On Being Human.*

[29] Lauretta Bender, "Genesis of Hostility in Children," *American Journal of Psychiatry,* Vol. 105 (1948), pp. 241–45.

[30] A. H. Maslow, "Our Maligned Animal Nature," *Journal of Psychology,* Vol. 28 (1949), pp. 273–78.

[31] *Ibid,* pp. 275–76.

[32] Karen Horney, *The Neurotic Personality of Our Time* (New York: Norton, 1937); Erich Fromm, *Man for Himself* (New York: Rinehart, 1947); Harry Stack Sullivan, *Conceptions of Modern Psychiatry* (Washington, D.C.: William Alanson White Psychiatric Foundation, 1952).

[33] "Our Maligned Animal Nature," p. 276.

[34] For some interesting comments bearing on these points see Geoffrey Gorer, "Some Notes on the British Character," *Horizon,* Vol. 20 (1949–50), pp. 369–79.

[35] In Johann G. Kohl, *England, Wales, and Scotland* (London: Chapman & Hall, 1844), p. 79.

[36] Supporting evidence will be found in M. F. Ashley Montagu, *Statement on Race,* 2d ed. (New York: Schuman, 1952); and in M. F. Ashley Montagu, *Man's Most Dangerous Myth: The Fallacy of Race.* See also booklets on race published by UNESCO.

[37] Joseph A. de Gobineau, *Essai sur l'inégalité des races humaines* (Paris, 1853–55); Houston Stewart Chamberlain, *Die Grundlagen des Neunzehntenjahrhunderts* (Berlin, 1900). For an excellent analysis of the racist writings of Richard Wagner, see Leon Stein, *The Racial Thinking of Richard Wagner* (New York: Philosophical Library, 1950).

[38] See Hannah Arendt, *The Origins of Totalitarianism* (New York: Harcourt, Brace & World, 1951); Frederick Hertz, *Nationality in History and Politics* (London: Kegan Paul, 1944).

[39] See particularly, Jean Finot, *Les Prejuje des Races* (Paris, 1905); English translation, *Race Prejudice* (Los Angeles: Zeitlin & Ver Brugge, 1906, 1945).

[40] T. W. Adorno, E. Frenkel-Brunswik, D. J. Levenson, and R. Nevitt Sanford, *The Authoritarian Personality* (New York: Harper and Row, 1950).

[41] Bruno Bettelheim and Morris Janowitz, "Prejudice," *Scientific*

American, Vol. 183 (1950), p. 13. See also the same authors' *Dynamics of Prejudice* (New York: Harper and Row, 1950).

⁴² Karl F. Schleussler and Donald R. Cressey, "Personality Characteristics of Criminals," *American Journal of Sociology,* Vol. 55 (1950), pp. 476–84.

⁴³ E. A. Hooton, *The American Criminal* (Cambridge, Mass.: Harvard University Press, 1939); E. A. Hooton, *Crime and the Man* (Cambridge, Mass.: Harvard University Press, 1939).

⁴⁴ *Crime and the Man,* p. 130.

⁴⁵ *Ibid.,* p. 397.

⁴⁶ For a more detailed criticism of Hooton's work see R. K. Merton and M. F. Ashley Montagu, "Crime and the Anthropologist," *American Anthropologist,* Vol. 42 (1940), pp. 384–408; see also W. A. Lessa, "An Appraisal of Constitutional Typologies," Memoir No. 62 of the American Anthropological Association, Vol. 45 (1943), p. 96.

⁴⁷ A full description of the method and findings will be found in W. H. Sheldon, *The Varieties of Human Physique* (New York: Harper and Row, 1940); and W. H. Sheldon, *The Varieties of Human Temperament* (New York: Harper and Row, 1942).

⁴⁸ Ernst Kretschmer, *Physique and Character* (New York: Harcourt, Brace & World, 1925).

⁴⁹ W. H. Sheldon, *Varieties of Delinquent Youth* (New York: Harper and Row, 1949).

⁵⁰ E. H. Sutherland, "Critique of Sheldon's Varieties of Delinquent Youth," *American Journal of Sociology,* Vol. 57 (1951), pp. 10–13.

⁵¹ *Varieties of Delinquent Youth,* pp. 842–43.

⁵² *Ibid.,* pp. 744–45.

⁵³ *Ibid.,* p. 830.

⁵⁴ *Ibid.,* p. 879.

Index